ENCOUNTER
THROUGH THE
BIBLE

JUDGES | RUTH | 1 & 2 SAMUEL

Copyright © Scripture Union 2011
First published 2011
ISBN 978 1 84427 576 2

Scripture Union England and Wales
207–209 Queensway, Bletchley, Milton Keynes MK2 2EB, UK
Email: info@scriptureunion.org.uk
Website: www.scriptureunion.org.uk

Scripture Union Australia
Locked Bag 2, Central Coast Business Centre, NSW 2252
Website: www.su.org.au

Scripture Union USA
PO Box 987, Valley Forge, PA 19482
Website: www.scriptureunion.org

The daily devotional notes for *Encounter through the Bible* have previously appeared in *Encounter with God*, a Scripture Union dated daily Bible guide.

The introductory material is adapted for this series from *The Bible in Outline* (Scripture Union, 1985) and *Explorer's Guide to the Bible* (John Grayston, Scripture Union, 2008).

British Library Cataloguing-in-Publication Data: a catalogue record of this book is available from the British Library.

Series editor: 'Tricia Williams
Printed and bound in India by Nutech Print Services
Cover design by Heather Knight

Scripture Union is an international Christian charity working with churches in more than 130 countries, providing resources to bring the good news about Jesus to children, young people and families and to encourage them to develop spiritually through the Bible and prayer. As well as co-ordinating a network of volunteers, staff and associates who run holidays, church-based events and school groups, we produce a wide range of publications and support those who use our resources through training programmes.

CONTENTS

MEETING GOD

For many years Christians throughout the world have found the 'Scripture Union method' a tremendous help in deepening their relationship with God as they read the Bible. Here is a modern version of that method, which aims to help you to make your time with God a true meeting with him. You may like to refer to it each day as a supplement to the comments in this volume.

COME TO GOD as you are. Worship him for his power, greatness and majesty. Bring him your feelings and needs. Ask for his Holy Spirit to help you understand and respond to what you read.

READ the Bible passage slowly and thoughtfully, listening out for what God is saying to you.

TALK WITH GOD about what you have read. These suggestions may help you:

- 'Lord, thank you for your Word to me today. What special message are you shouting out to me, or whispering to me, in these verses?'

- 'Lord, I want to meet you here; tell me more about yourself, Father, Son and Holy Spirit, in these verses.'

- 'I don't know what today holds for me, Lord. I need your guidance, your advice. I need you to help me be alert. Direct my heart and thoughts to those words you know I need.'

- 'Lord, your Word is a mirror in which I often find myself. Show me myself here, as you see me, alone or with others. Thank you that you understand how I feel as I read your Word.'

- 'Lord, there are things here I don't understand. Please help me through the notes in this guide, or give me others who may help me.'

RESPOND Try to find a key thought or phrase which has come to you from this passage to carry with you through the day. Pray for people who are on your mind at the moment. Determine to share your experiences with others.

USING THIS GUIDE

Encounter through the Bible is a devotional Bible guide that can be used any time. It uses some of the best of the *Encounter with God* Bible series to guide the reader through whole Bible books in a systematic way. Like *Encounter with God*, it is designed for thinking Christians who want to interpret and apply the Bible in a way that is relevant to the problems and issues of today's world.

It is hoped that eventually the series will lead readers through the whole Bible. This volume covers Judges, Ruth and 1 & 2 Samuel. Look out for the other guides available now:

Old Testament
Genesis, Exodus, Leviticus
Numbers, Deuteronomy, Joshua

New Testament
Matthew, Mark
Luke, John

The notes are arranged in Bible book order – in this volume, Judges to 2 Samuel. Each Bible book series begins with an introduction giving an overview of the book and its message. These aim to help you to get a grip on the book as a whole.

Each daily note begins with a call to worship which should help you consciously come into God's presence before you read the passage. The main 'explore' section aims to bring out the riches hidden in the text. The response section at the end of the note may include prayer or praise and suggest ways of applying the message to daily living.

JUDGES

Judges provides the link between Joshua, who led Israel into Canaan, and Saul, David and the other kings of Israel. The 12 'judges' were not merely concerned with legal matters; they were princes inspired by the Holy Spirit to give a charismatic kind of leadership in times of need. They recognised that they led by divine will, not merely by human choice. Judges tells the stories of the 12 judges and six periods of oppression. A cycle of events becomes apparent:

1) All is going well for the people.

2) They forget about God and pagan gods of their neighbours take his place. Oppression is the result. God abandons them to their own ways. Moab and Ammon, the Philistines and the Midianites all in turn attack Israel.

3) Israel repents and asks for forgiveness. Each time God is willing to forgive and restore.

4) Then, a judge appears who delivers his people. Each time it is made clear that it is God who saves, through the judge.

5) All is going well for the people... and so the sin-cycle starts again.

Judges teaches us that man without God is helpless. The book of Judges gives us an unmistakable object lesson, showing us our need of a Saviour. The faith of the judges was commended by the writer of Hebrews,[1] yet as Christians we can rejoice for the promise that we have received through Jesus: '... only together with us would they be made perfect.'[2]

Outline

1 The invasion of Canaan	1:1 - 2:5
2 Rule of the 12 judges	2:6 - 16:31
3 A historical miscellany	17:1 - 21:25

[1] Heb 11:32–34 [2] Heb 11:40

PROMISING BEGINNINGS

We believe in a God of fresh starts. Thank the Lord that his love is 'new every morning',[1] even when we have been guilty of indifference or failure.

JUDGES 1:1–26

When did you last undertake a new project? Take a moment to revisit the emotions involved, and recall how your initial plans were modified as the project developed. This will help you identify with today's passage, which recounts a new wave of conquest. Under Joshua the initial raids in the centre, the south and the north (Joshua 6, 10 and 11 respectively) had been successful, and the whole land was divided among the tribes. But much remained unconquered (Joshua 13-19).[2] So this was a new, later project. The key tribes were Judah and Simeon, who then settled together and (with Benjamin) formed the later kingdom of Judah. They alone survived the exile and returned as Jews to Judea, which was of course the nation of Jesus. So our faith has historical roots in this passage!

The basic narrative notes the capture of what were probably the main towns in the whole southern area: Bezek (near Gezer, v 4), Jerusalem (v 8; though lost again later, v 21), Hebron (v 10), Debir (v 11), Hormah (v 17), three western towns (later ruled by the Philistines, v 18) and Bethel (v 22). This campaign was certainly successful. Then there are also some subsidiary stories about Adoni-Bezek (vs 5-7), Caleb (vs 12-15), Moses' in-laws (v 16) and a collaborator from Bethel (vs 23-26). Each story gives a little cameo, reminding us of the many complexities of life.

What can we learn here about how to approach new ventures? The first verse provides the spiritual key to this passage: the people sought the Lord, who responded (v 2), and repeatedly gave them victory (vs 4,19,22). These promising beginnings came from an attitude of faith, along with perseverance to see the task through and flexibility to make adjustments en route. How might this apply to you and your church?

Lord, help me to keep going through thick and thin.[3]

[1] Lam 3:23 [2] Note Josh 13:1 [3] See 1 Cor 15:58

THE PLOT UNRAVELS

'Forgive us our sins...' What specific sins have you recently confessed? What have you done since, both to make amends and to avoid repetition? Reflect quietly before God.

JUDGES 1:27 – 2:5

This section is dominated by a sorry catalogue of failure, as tribe after tribe 'did not drive out' the local peoples.[1] Some tribes partially subdued them, but others didn't even manage that. So the positive report of success in the southern half of the country (vs 1–26) is immediately countered by this serially negative one in the north.

Two details are worth noting. First, the restriction to the hills noted for the Danites (v 34) was actually more widespread. Indigenous Canaanites and invading groups occupied the more fertile plains and valleys, while the Israelites were forced into the less productive hills. Second, the generalised references to times of Israelite strength (vs 28,35) show a later summary of this uneven period. Christians similarly pass through periods of marginalisation and of strength. How would you describe your local or national context?

The section concludes with its theological key, presented by an unnamed 'messenger' of the Lord. (Most Bibles translate this as 'angel', but the Hebrew term simply means messenger, whether supernatural or human. This divine messenger probably appeared in human form, since the other two such 'messengers' in the book seem human until they disappear.[2]) God and Israel had a covenant, a formal treaty with mutual obligations. Israel had broken this covenant, yet God declares he will not abandon it, but only revise the terms. He would still be their God, but would not complete the conquest for them. The people respond with tears and sacrifice, but apparently not much else. Unlike the revival in Samuel's time,[3] there was no practical response in destroying the pagan altars. While some may have been sincere, for the majority this looks more like remorse than repentance.

So what about your recent confession to God? Was it sterile remorse or fertile repentance?[4]

[1] 1:27,29,30,31,33 [2] See Judg 6:21; 13:20 [3] 1 Sam 7:4 [4] 2 Cor 7:9,10

A SORRY CYCLE

Joshua's godly leadership influenced a whole generation. Thank God for the Joshuas of your generation, and for their influence on your own life.

JUDGES 2:6 – 3:6

This looks like a new introduction to the book of Judges, repeating material from the end of Joshua[1] before summarising the contents of Judges. Overlap and double introduction are typical features of biblical literature, and remind us that the authors were less concerned with literary polish and more with spiritual message. And what a message to open this section! Joshua's leadership extended beyond his lifetime, as a whole younger generation who witnessed the conquest remained faithful to the Lord. So often in biblical and Christian history, when a dynamic leader moves on their good work unravels – can you think of modern examples? Not so Joshua. Though he often seems overshadowed by Moses, he actually receives a tribute which equals that of his great mentor.

But sadly a new generation arises in ignorance both of the Lord and of his deeds. As Christians we are lopsided if we have a good relationship with God but little interest in our Christian heritage, or vice versa. Unfortunately these Israelites were doubly ignorant, and fell away from the one true God to worship local Baals and Ashtoreths. These are general terms for male and female deities respectively, and each would have had a local name.[2] All were forbidden.

So began the sorry cycle, recounted in verses 12-19: apostasy, oppression, a judge, deliverance, the judge's death, renewed apostasy, oppression, and so on. But this isn't just the ebb and flow of history. The text repeatedly emphasises both divine initiative (vs 14-16,18) and human failing (vs 12,13,17,19). Each time there is opportunity for other choices. Each time, though, God acts in grace towards a wayward people. It's the story of so much of Scripture, of Christian history and of our own lives.

You are probably (by God's grace) more like faithful Joshua than the faithless people. Pray about your own influence over others.

[1] Josh 24:28–31 [2] See Num 25:3

MAJOR AND MINOR JUDGES?

Today, recall some of the many Christians who have had a significant influence on your life. Thank God for the rich communion of saints.

JUDGES 3:7–11,31

The judges are often divided into two groups, with six called 'major' because we have stories of their exploits, and the other six 'minor' because we know very little about them. Today's verses introduce us to the first of each group – yet both are untypical. Othniel is the major judge with the shortest story, and Shamgar is the only minor judge with an account of a military exploit. Immediately our simple classification breaks down, reminding us to beware of pigeonholing people.

The first story has all the elements of the typical cycle in Judges: apostasy, oppression, cry for help, a judge, deliverance and a period of peace. The formidable-sounding Cushan-Rishathaim is otherwise unknown, and probably came from the north-east but had settled locally (Aram-Naharaim normally refers to territory beyond the distant Euphrates). By contrast, Othniel was noted earlier for capturing Debir (and, along with it, a wife!).[1] Here again he rises to the challenge and brings freedom for a generation. His exploit may have a shorter account than for the other major judges, but its effect lasted longer than for many. Again, we must beware of appearances.

At the end of the chapter is the single verse on Shamgar. By contrast with the above, it lacks virtually all the elements of a typical judge story. But it does have the one key ingredient: he saved Israel. This highlights a central aspect of the judges: they were first and foremost deliverers, and only consequently leaders (or judges). Shamgar's renown was later celebrated,[2] and he presages Samson in both the type of weapon used and the enemies fought,[3] but here we have only the briefest account. In this he reminds us of the many Christian heroes about whom we know very little, but whose faith and faithfulness we celebrate.

Look back at a biography that challenged you when you first read it. Allow God to renew that challenge, and to prompt you to new service.

[1] Judg 1:13 [2] Judg 5:6 [3] Judg 15:14

EHUD THE LEFTIE

'It is God who arms me with strength and keeps my way secure.'[1]

This next story about a judge brings us to a more familiar enemy. The Moabites were Israel's distant cousins,[2] with territory east of the Dead Sea. They had first been hostile when Israel wanted to pass through on their way to the Promised Land, despite the latter's peaceful approach.[3] They then went much further in enticing Israel into idolatry and immorality at Baal Peor, resulting in divinely sanctioned Israelite vengeance.[4] Here the two groups are at enmity again, and Moab has the upper hand, invading and capturing Jericho. How often our enemies, temptations and sins are familiar rather than new!

This time the deliverer is a man called Ehud, and the first thing we are told about him is that he's a 'leftie'. Even in our own times left-handed people have known discrimination, being forced to use their right hand to write and do all sorts of tasks they find difficult. All the more so in the ancient world. So Ehud may have had to overcome various difficulties – and overcome them he certainly did! Ehud's left-handedness is vital to the story, since it means he can conceal a sword where it's not expected. And he turns this to good use, inventing a reason for a private audience with Moab's king and then killing him. Of course it was a risk, but he took it, and led Israel to victory and an unequalled 80 years of peace.

As a leftie myself, I can identify with Ehud. The fact is we are all different in some way, we all have some things in our lives which we can see as an obstacle. The question is not so much what they are, but what we do about them. Do they hinder us, or can we see some way God can use them for his glory?[5]

Do you have some seeming flaw which makes you feel awkward? Ask God to turn this apparent weakness into an opportunity.

---

[1] 2 Sam 22:33 [2] Gen 19:37 [3] Deut 2:9; Judg 11:17 [4] Num 25,31 [5] 2 Cor 4:7–10; 6:10; 12:7–10

A TALE OF TWO WOMEN

Where would you least like God to send you to live and work? Ponder before God how you would react to such a call.

JUDGES 4

Hazor means little to most of us – just another ancient town. But it meant an awful lot to early Israelites! Located north of the Sea of Galilee, it was the largest Canaanite city throughout the second millennium BC, frequently mentioned in Egyptian and Mesopotamian records. It dominated the surrounding area, physically and politically. Its king, Jabin, marshalled resistance to Joshua, but he was defeated and Hazor destroyed.[1] However, it then recovered and another Jabin now ruled the roost. No wonder Barak was fearful of attacking its army. But Deborah had no such fear. Despite the restrictions on women in ancient Israel (and the ancient world generally), she was recognised as prophet and judge (v 4, literal reading).There is no record that she was a hero-deliverer like the other major judges, so she may have become a judge because of the leadership she exercised in prophecy. That leadership is certainly clear in this story, where she is not afraid to confront the dominant power. Barak leads Israel's army to a famous rout of Sisera's forces, but the true victor is clearly Deborah. So let Deborah be your inspiration in overcoming restrictions!

The other heroine is less expected, in that her Kenite family were allies of Hazor. Perhaps Moses' in-laws hadn't really integrated into Israel, but Jael uses this to her advantage, luring Sisera to a false sense of security before despatching him with a tent peg. Like Rahab, she abandoned family loyalties to side with God's people, even though they were often unfaithful. As well as sealing this famous victory, her actions may have helped the gradual integration of the Kenites into Israel.[2] These two women certainly saved Israel. Now as then, God works through both recognised leaders and other believers. Whichever you are, be open to his prompting and courageous in your response.

Godly initiative can come from unexpected quarters. Have you dismissed any ideas recently because they didn't come from recognised leaders?

[1] Josh 11:1,10 [2] See 1 Chr 2:55

COME ON, LET'S CELEBRATE!

As you approach God today, sing to yourself a song or hymn celebrating your salvation. Take time to sing it all, and to enjoy it!

There's something profoundly human about wanting to sing, whether on the football terraces or just at home in the bath. We like to sing - especially when we want to celebrate! Christians have been renowned for their songs, in every era and every culture. In the Old Testament, too, there are many songs: nationally after deliverance from Egypt, personally for Hannah and Hezekiah,[1] and, of course, the whole book of Psalms.

Judges 5 is a glorious psalm of victory, with many pointed contrasts. In the bad old days the Israelites took to the hills, but now they can go down to the city gates (vs 6-11). Some tribes risked their lives willingly, while others sat on their hands (vs 13-18,23). The enemy kings were mighty, but the forces they faced were mightier (vs 19-22). Jael was a heroine, Sisera's mother a mourner (vs 24-30). Like many a biblical hymn[2] it celebrates God's reversal, his lifting up of the humble, his choosing the weak and lowly.

Two other themes mark this song. There is joyful praise to the Lord, who gave the victory. It was he, the awesome God of Sinai, who sent sudden rain, making the ground difficult for chariots, and caused swollen rivers, sweeping them away (vs 4,5,20,21). It was God who wrought victory against his enemies (v 31). There is also repeated reference to those who volunteer and fight willingly (vs 2,9,13-15,18). In the judges period the Israelite tribes were often hostile to each other, whereas here at least some of them worked together. In the Christian world, we too will see God at work more wonderfully when we learn to stop bickering and work together for our common goal - spreading the good news of transformation in Christ.

'May all who love you be like the sun when it rises in its strength' (v 31). Celebration leads to renewed commitment – what about yours?

---

[1] Exod 15:1–18; 1 Sam 2:1–10; Isa 38:10–20 [2] eg Luke 1:46–55

GROWING FAITH

Think back to your first bold steps of faith, and relive the experience. Thank God for his enabling, and worship him as all-powerful.

JUDGES 6

This chapter subdivides into four sections. First (vs 1–10) there's a general introduction to this period, noting the usual cycle of apostasy, oppression and cry for help, with the variation of God's response through a prophet. Then (vs 11–24) there's Gideon's first encounter with God. As before, 'angel' should be translated 'messenger', since Gideon didn't realise the messenger was supernatural until his disappearance (v 22). The early exchange is stirring, with some memorable affirmations (vs 12,14). Why does God often use people lacking in self-confidence?[1] Having been reassured that he won't die, Gideon gives his altar a name remarkable for the times. In our similarly troubled days we also need to find imaginative ways to proclaim, 'The LORD is peace.' Third (vs 25–32), Gideon obeys God and confronts the local community, demolishing their pagan worship site and building a substitute. Though he acts by night, the results are immediately apparent and bring recrimination. Surprisingly, Gideon's father seems unfazed by the loss of an ox and his personal altar, and wisely defuses the stand-off, rather like Gamaliel.[2] Sometimes bold witness receives support from surprising quarters. As we remember Gideon and the apostles, may we too learn to act with courage.

Finally (vs 33–40), he summons the local militia and conducts his famous fleece tests. Divinely commissioned and paternally encouraged, he musters the threatened Israelites to face the invading hordes. Then he needs further reassurance. God graciously grants this, and the scene is set for the showdown. Was he right to put out his fleece? He isn't rebuked for it. Should we 'put out a fleece'? Why not? It may be a way in which God guides us. What is important is what we do consequently.

Bring to God a decision you're wrestling with, asking for clear direction and resolving to follow it.

---

[1] *See eg,* Exod 3:11; Jer 1:6 [2] *See* Acts 5:35–39

DIVINE MATHS

Recall some of the many ways God has made himself known to you, perhaps including dreams, and open yourself to him for fresh anointing.

'We're too few!' How easy it is to think this, and to be jealous of large churches. 'They have all the resources, so let them get on with winning the world for Christ – we haven't, so we can't.' Today's passage seriously challenges such negative thinking and unbiblical perceptions.

A sizeable army of some 32,000 men gathered – far short of the innumerable invaders (v 12), but still a decent number. Yet there were too many for God. All the fearful were to go home, and only one out of every three stayed. Still, at least all those left were courageous, and could count on each other. But there were still too many for God – and at the second round only one of every 33 was retained! Perhaps they were particularly astute, drinking on their feet to remain alert. But what on earth could a mere 300 do?

Given this unexpected turn of events, it's hardly surprising that Gideon needed further reassurance, so God let him overhear a Midianite's dream. Throughout history God has used dreams to speak to people.[1] I still remember one from my teenage years, in which a cross-shaped shadow passed over our school assembly and a voice from heaven challenged me. Here the dream seems to have galvanised Gideon into action. No one expected armies to attack at night, so the sudden blaze of lights around the camp and the cacophony of trumpet blasts panicked the invaders into fighting each other. The small number was crucial to maintain surprise – and of course it emphasised that the victory was entirely God's.[2] So those of us in small churches with a struggling witness need to count our blessings and look again to God to do amazing things through a small but dedicated group.

Ask forgiveness for allowing a small cause to make you either complacent or desperate, and take heart from Gideon's 300!

[1] Num 12:6: Dan 5:12; Matt 1:20; Acts 2:17 [2] 2 Chr 20:15; Isa 48:11

DISSENT AND CORRUPTION

Thank God for the rich and vibrant diversity of the church, and for all you've learnt from other groups and denominations.

JUDGES 8

How quickly dissent creeps into the ranks! First there is a quarrel with the touchy Ephraimites, who resented being left out of the initial action. The most northerly tribes had been summoned (6:35), but Ephraim was a little further south. Gideon skilfully appeases them with a little flattery (vs 1–3). Then two Israelite towns east of the Jordan and more exposed to Midianite raids are wary of supporting their fellow countrymen. This time, by contrast, Gideon promises terrible retribution (vs 7,9). So the euphoria of victory is tempered by internal bickering and non-cooperation. This of course was typical of the Judges period – we noted the incomplete support for Deborah and Barak (ch 5), and will see it further with the Ephraimites and Jephthah (12:1–6), and at its worst in the tragic final story (chs 19–21). The same has been sadly typical of much church history. When many Western churches are in decline, we need to ask if one main reason is our touchiness and refusal to cooperate effectively.

But just as bad – how quickly power corrupts the leader! Gideon acted generously towards the Ephraimites, but harshly in punishing the men of Succoth and Peniel (vs 16,17).[1] Gideon was single-minded in achieving the divinely given victory over the Midianites, but his execution of their kings seems motivated more by personal revenge (v 19). Most importantly of all, Gideon was wise in refusing kingship, but incredibly foolish in taking a tax on the spoils to make his own idol. So one stupendous victory, achieved by divine guidance and providence, has led this timid man first to bold faith but then all too quickly to brazen self-importance. In our own days how sad to hear, and that all too frequently, of the fall of Christian leaders, whose success has gone to their heads.

'If you think you are standing firm, be careful that you don't fall!'[2] Pray this through for yourself, and your church leaders. Could friendships of mutual accountability help to keep us all from falling?

[1] Even Saul was able to forgive early opposition; *see* 1 Sam 11:13   [2] 1 Cor 10:12

THE THORNBUSH

Thank God for Christian values of human worth, and for the freedoms that many of us enjoy. Express penitence that often our blessings lead us astray.

It is sometimes true that people get the leaders they deserve. Here we see the seeds of sin beginning to bear terrible fruit in Gideon's sexual greed – excessive even for a leader – in having a concubine as well as many wives, his irreverent giving of their son a name meaning 'my father is king' (8:30,31), Abimelek's lust for power, and the Shechemites' desire for influence. It all leads to the slaughter of Gideon's legitimate offspring, a unilateral declaration of kingship by two towns, and Abimelek exercising rule over at least part of Israel for three years (v 22), no doubt with the viciousness shown elsewhere in the story. The devil is certainly happy to work long term. Sowing to please our sinful nature will reap a terrible harvest.[1]

But one son escapes and challenges the rebels from a rocky crag before fleeing for his life. Tree imagery was commonplace,[2] and the point of this parable is that the good trees refuse kingship, while the harmful thorn-bush insists that mighty cedars stoop down to it or get burned up by its rage. Jotham's 'if' (vs 16,19) is obviously rhetorical – the Shechemites have not been fair to his family, so the upstart king and his self-made kingdom will consume each other. For a few years this prediction seems a mere fable, but then mutual mistrust and antagonism set in, and the parable comes dreadfully true.

This all seems remote from the world in which many of us live – until we remember that all it takes for evil to flourish is for good people to do nothing.[3] We live in a world where honesty, integrity and respect are increasingly absent. Could we make a greater effort to practise these values ourselves? Could we do more to make it clear to politicians and others that we want leaders who prize these values?

Pray about these issues in your own context of work, home and friendships. Ask for wisdom to know what to address and how, and for courage to stand up for what is right.

[1] Gal 6:7,8 [2] *See* 2 Kings 14:9, and texts like Isa 1:30; 2:13; 4:2 [3] Edmund Burke, political theorist, 1729–97

YOU REAP WHAT YOU SOW?

Many people think that you get what you deserve in life. Praise the Lord that because of his grace this is not true for us!

JUDGES 9:26–57

Abimelek and the Shechemites have sown the wind and reaped the whirlwind, to quote Hosea's later description of Israel.[1] The outsider Gaal stirs up dissent in Shechem, its governor Zebul reports this to Abimelek, and he then slaughters Gaal and his crowd. Not content with this, he proceeds to massacre all Shechem's farmers, then destroy the city, and finally burn down its fortified tower with the thousand poor people inside. The thorn-bush's fire consumes them all,[2] some literally. And the fire spreads, as Abimelek then attacks Thebez. Did he suspect them of complicity, or was this wanton cruelty to terrorise everyone else, as practised by tyrants from time immemorial? We are not told. But here the fire he had started consumed Abimelek himself, in fulfilment of Jotham's parable.

Sometimes, though not always, people do get what they deserve in life. Abimelek and the Shechemites certainly did. The Mosaic law predicted happy prosperity for a community obedient to God and dreadful misery for a disobedient one,[3] and this seems to have been the general experience through later history, with increased misery in the judges period, growing prosperity under David and Solomon, and mixed experience in the kingdoms of Israel and Judah until both were swept into exile. But the key phrase is 'the general experience'. In this story, as so often in history (and still today), many others were caught up in dreadful events without being directly responsible for them. Like the Law, the Psalms and Proverbs present a case for obedience leading to blessing – but other psalms[4] and the book of Job warn us not to absolutise these principles. There are many innocent sufferers. Above all, the whole basis of Scripture is that God doesn't treat believers as we deserve, but offers us his grace instead.

James asserts that, 'Mercy triumphs over judgement'.[5] Ask God to show you how you can let mercy trump judgement in your sphere of influence.

[1] Hos 8:7   [2] Judg 9:15   [3] Lev 26; Deut 28   [4] eg Pss 37; 73   [5] James 2:13

THE WIDER PICTURE

Think about a country or context other than your own where the church has experienced repentance and revival, and praise the Lord for this.

JUDGES 10

After mentioning two minor judges, this passage is the most detailed religious account since the opening chapters. We have a long list of illicit deities, including for the first time those of north-west Sidon (in Phoenicia, modern Lebanon) and north-east Aram (ie Syria). Their worship leads predictably to further oppression and an Israelite cry of distress, but this time the story is different in two ways. First, God reminds them of past deliverances, which they have now ignored, and challenges them to seek help from their new gods. Then the Israelites recognise their failure and show genuine repentance in removing these foreign gods. This sets the scene for the next judge, Jephthah. So right here, in the heart of this depressing book, there is potential for renewal. This can give us fresh hope as we look out on and intercede for our own deeply troubled world.

It is interesting to step back from today's passage and note the northern and eastern locations of most of the judges and campaigns. Only two were based in the south, Ibzan of Bethlehem,[1] and Othniel of Debir,[2] and two fought the Philistines in the south-west, Shamgar[3] and Samson.[4] All the others came from or fought foes from the north or the east. Even at this early stage in Israel's history, the northern tribes were more prone to apostasy. They were more exposed to foreign influence and invasion, and in religious terms they let many Canaanites and their cults survive (1:27–30) and were then led astray by them. There was potential for true revival then, and later under Samuel and David, but it failed to have lasting effect, and the northern tribes were eventually disbursed in exile, never to regroup. As we too face many cultural and religious pressures, we need a radical repentance that is not short-lived.

Ask God for renewed hope in your intercession, and a long-term vision in your witness.

---

[1] 12:8 [2] 1:11–13, though his deliverance is not localised, 3:9–11 [3] 3:31
[4] Chs 13–16

LEADER FROM NOWHERE

Worship the Lord who calls the weak and lowly, and who constantly challenges our views of human value.

JUDGES 11:1–28

Another story of a prostitute's son, of animosity between him and his half-brothers, of a gang of 'scoundrels'.[1] It all leads us to expect another horrific account like that of Abimelek – but it doesn't turn out that way. In their plight, the eastern Gileadites appeal to Jephthah, whose response is most surprising: no requirement of revenge on his hostile brothers, or on the town generally; no delight in their current predicament; no insistence on hefty pre-payment. All he requests is what he needs to do the job – the promise of headship, solemnly sworn before the Lord (vs 9–11). Jephthah rises above his unpromising beginnings to exhibit true statesmanship. How often do we judge people according to their background, and expect Abimeleks rather than Jephthahs?

Jephthah then confronts the Ammonite king with a history lesson. Before Israel entered Canaan, it captured a large stretch of land, east of the lower Jordan and the Dead Sea, from Sihon of the Amorites (note carefully the different name).[2] The Ammonites had then been living further north and east but they had since expanded and wanted to claim this territory, so Jephthah reminded him that it had been Israelite for centuries and told him that they would defend it. Indeed, their God would judge the dispute (vs 26,27). Again, Jephthah shows his leadership by knowing and quoting history, and by his faith that the Lord of the past was still the Lord of the present. So an outcast outlaw is emboldened to challenge an invader in the Lord's name. Whether due to the recent revival,[3] divine anointing (v 29), his personal faith, or all three, Jephthah's trust and courage present a refreshing change in this unhappy period. Again, how often do we too quickly judge certain contexts and situations (political or religious) as beyond redemption?

Remind yourself what God has done in the past in your church, and share with others the vision that this is the same God we serve today.

[1] So TNIV, v 3 [2] Deut 2:24–37 [3] Judg 10:16

TRIUMPH AND TRAGEDY

Praise God that we do not have to earn his acceptance or assistance by making vows.

JUDGES 11:29 – 12:7

Jephthah achieved a famous victory. Endowed with God's Spirit, he routed the powerful Ammonites and successfully defended all the disputed territory, from Gilead in the north to Aroer at its southern edge. Later on, the Ammonites captured the land and established their capital at Rabbath Ammon (modern Amman).This was the town David later declined to fight, with disastrous consequences.[1] But for now Jephthah preserved Israel's heritage. Then he dealt with the quarrelsome Ephraimites, who again wanted the easy spoils.[2] Jephthah was in no mood for appeasement, and they were slaughtered as they fled, with their dialect betraying their identity – the original shibboleth.

But sadly, like Richard Nixon and many others, Jephthah is remembered more for tragedy than triumph. Before battle he made a rash vow – what on earth could he have been thinking? And now in his moment of triumphant return, a nightmare unfolds, and his precious only daughter must become a sacrificial victim. It has been argued that the sacrifice consisted of her remaining a virgin, never marrying. But this evades the natural meaning of the passage, and hardly accounts for the annual four-day mourning to commemorate the poor girl. Despite his faith, Jephthah obviously had a limited understanding of the Lord, and assumed he need to make a costly vow in order to gain the victory. What tragic ignorance.

Arthur Cundall concludes appropriately: 'The incident witnesses to the sacredness of a vow undertaken before the Lord ... and we must at least respect this man and his daughter who were loyal, at such a cost, to their limited beliefs. There comes the challenge to the modern reader, whose knowledge of God is much greater than that of Jephthah, to offer to Him a comparable but enlightened loyalty.'[3]

Think of Christian leaders associated with tragedy, whatever the cause, and pray for them.

[1] 2 Sam 11:1 [2] As in Judg 8:1 [3] AE Cundall and L Morris, *Judges and Ruth*, TOTC; IVP, 1981, p149

LESSONS FROM THE PAST

Thank God for our rich heritage of Christian thought, life and witness.

JUDGES 12:8–15

Why does the inspired human author record the story of these minor judges, although he probably knows only a few details about them from his sources? Several such leaders are mentioned. Along with Ibzan, Elon and Abdon listed here, we can include Tola and Jair in 10:1-5 and remember the valiant Shamgar of 3:31. We note these judges' numerous progeny – Jair, Ibzan and Abdon had 100 sons between them (though fewer each than Gideon's 70 sons)[1] – and their wealth, since the rich rode donkeys (as Deborah's song records).[2] This implies recognition of their status by the local tribes. We note too that the length of their rule is recorded precisely, rather than the (probably) round figures of 20, 40 and 80 years for most major judges. This suggests that the detail, though scanty, is carefully recorded. Furthermore, we note that some of these men brought stability for long periods: Tola and Jair led/judged Israel for over two decades, much longer than Jephthah.

Perhaps the biggest lesson of all, however, is the very paucity of detail. These were leaders raised up by God in difficult times, who kept powerful enemies at bay and brought a measure of peace in troubled times. I'm struck by the many similarities with Christian history, in the past and in our own times. Though not a historian, I really enjoyed studying church history at college and getting glimpses into the faith and witness of many saints, now largely forgotten, and I've always enjoyed reading Christian biographies, especially the more honest ones, as they bring that rich history up to date. So we can learn from these 'minor' judges, and from many other forgotten witnesses, that God can use even us to fulfil his purposes, and that our work for him will not be in vain[3] or forgotten.[4]

Use a coming evening or weekend to read about Christian saints of the past, whether ancient or recent. Then ask yourself, 'What mark will I leave?'

[1] Judg 8:30 [2] Judg 5:10 [3] 1 Cor 15:58 [4] Rev 14:13

A NEW DELIVERER?

'I'm homesick – longing for your salvation; I'm waiting for your word of hope.'[1] Recall a time when God left you in discomfort.

Samson came from Dan, the tribe assigned south-west Canaan. Even before all the tribes were settled, the Danites were finding it hard to hold on to their inheritance as gradually the Amorites, pressured by the Philistines expanding from their coastal domain, pushed into their territory. The text suggests[2] that the Danites were already living on the margins of their tribal area in camps, facing full expulsion.

Meanwhile, 'the People of Israel were back at it again, doing what was evil' (v 1, *The Message*). Another 'judge' was needed. In the promise of this 'deliverer', there are some parallels with the coming of Jesus, the ultimate deliverer. A messenger announces Samson's birth (vs 3,7,13) and his mother responds in faith. Samson's role was not to have the nationwide authority of the fourth judge, Deborah, or the saving military leadership of the fifth judge, Gideon. He was to waken the people out of the stupor into which they had fallen as they capitulated to the Philistines' invasion. Israel had sold out to the values of the infiltrators, and the Lord prepared Samson[3] to stir his people to resistance once again, lest this ungodly enemy take over the whole Promised Land. As we face up to massive church decline in much of the West, we too need to pray for strong leaders who will issue an unforgettable wake-up call.

In the cycle of rebellion, retribution, repentance and rescue that characterises Judges,[4] rebellion and retribution are present again but there is no sign here of either repentance or rescue. Even a Nazirite vow[5] does not seem to mean much. Samson's role is to bring the possibility of final apostasy into the open and to disturb the status quo, not to comfort the oppressed. The Philistine threat would not be removed until Samuel, Saul, Jonathan and finally David completed the task.[6]

Is God using discontent, like the stirring to resistance Samson prompted, to open you to something new?

1 Ps 119:81, *The Message* 2 v 25; also Cundall, pp160,161 3 *See* 14:4 4 M Wilcock, *The Message of Judges*, IVP, p126 5 Num 6:1–12 6 2 Sam 5:17–25

QUESTIONABLE PURITY

Prepare your heart with this paraphrase of Psalm 51:10: 'God, make a fresh start in me, shape a Genesis week from the chaos of my life.'[1]

JUDGES 14

When modern parents name their son 'Samson', I sometimes wonder if they have read the biblical story! On the surface, the Samson saga is a titillating tale of a man entranced by three beautiful women. But the blame for Samson's promiscuity does not primarily rest with the women. For someone under a Nazirite vow, Samson showed precious little discipline in his personal life, not unlike many Christians today. In his case, his indiscipline included touching dead carcasses and lingering in taboo vineyards.[2] As a Hebrew, he should also have known better than to enter into a liaison with a Philistine girl in clear disregard for both the covenant law and the wishes of his parents. But the disruption caused by his philandering works for God's purposes in stirring the Hebrews' resistance, for the main point of this chapter is the slaughter of the Philistines at Ashkelon.

What, then, are we to make of the references to 'the Spirit of the LORD' coming upon Samson?[3] Jesus taught us to know his Spirit as the Holy Spirit,[4] yet God's servant in this story is hardly holy. Samson was a man of his times, and the times were evil and lawless. As members of the tribe of Dan, his family were insecure in their tenure of the land and distant geographically from any central religious influence.[5] Yet his parents recognised God's messenger and knew how to respond to his presence and command. Is there any excuse for Samson's behaviour? The text suggests a hidden dynamic in the situation (v 4), though we are left with many questions. I was recently teaching pastors in a country very different from my own, once again aware how careful we need to be in condemning behaviour that is culturally different from our own. Samson was clearly less than a godly version of his own culture yet God still worked through him. Who are we to question God's purposes?

Today we may still find it difficult to understand why God uses certain individuals. Ask for grace to 'judge nothing before the appointed time'.[6]

[1] Ps 51:10, *The Message* [2] Num 6:3,6–8 [3] 13:25; 14:19 [4] John 14:26; *cf* 1 Thess 4:8 [5] *See* ch 17 [6] 1 Cor 4:5

NOTICE GOD AT WORK

'If your heart is broken, you'll find God right there; if you're kicked in the gut, he'll help you catch your breath.'[1]

We are meant to be impressed with Samson's strength. His fellow Israelites certainly were (v 11): 3,000 men to capture one? But then someone who can single-handedly slay 30 (14:19), set 300 burning foxes among the corn (15:4) or lay out 1,000 with the jawbone of a donkey (v 15) is to be taken seriously! The Israelites too would one day be taken seriously again and the land would finally be secured as promised to Abraham, but here it is still early days. Verses 9–12 are probably the lowest point in Israel's chequered history. The nation is not only completely powerless before an enemy taking away their beloved Promised Land, they do not even see any hope of rescue, not even through Samson with his God-given strength.

At other points in Israel's story we may well admire the Hebrews' tenacity in defending their land. Sometimes, as they did at this point, we feel helpless in the face of concerted opposition. In Western countries we fear that the influence of the Christian faith is on the wane. Have we lost hope? The growth of Christianity in Africa and South America, for example, should stir us to renewed confidence in the gospel.

On the other hand, if there is no conflict between us and the world, we have been lulled into complacency. 'Live and let live' may be a comfortable postmodern slogan for tolerance in societies where there are no longer firm values, but it is not God's perspective. Jesus warned, 'I have come to bring ... a sword'[2] and taught that the Holy Spirit would 'convict the world concerning sin'.[3] It was a commitment to both holiness and courage that led Joshua into the land,[4] and this spirit must be ours as we contend in God's name for his way.

How do you balance realism about your situation and hope in God working all things together for good?[5]

---

[1] Ps 34:18, *The Message* [2] Matt 10:34 [3] John 16:8–11, ESV [4] Josh 1:6–9
[5] Rom 8:28

DOING WHAT IS REQUIRED

The psalmist reminds us: 'You're blessed when you stay on course, walking steadily on the road revealed by GOD.'[1]

JUDGES 16:1–17

'The man whose great strength made him a legend in his own lifetime was completely unable to bridle his own passions.'[2] It could be a description of a rock star or a champion athlete, and in some ways Samson was both. Yet, as for many of our popular heroes, his stardom made him oblivious to reality. Why was he down in Gaza? Even if ordinary Israelites could merge into the local community, surely Samson couldn't, not with his reputation. And despite his initial caution, leaving unexpectedly in the middle of the night from the second woman, his hubris led to his downfall, as we see all too often today. The mighty gates of the city on display some distance away for all to see (v 3) were a spit in the eye of the Philistines, to which they felt they had to respond. Then the third Philistine woman, the famous Delilah, enters the story.

Again, the irony of the situation Israel has created is that Samson stands for Israel itself – the same predicament, the same blindness, the same unfaithfulness, potentially the same result. Like Samson, the nation too would not learn from previous experience.

We are told that Samson the judge was 'leading' Israel through all this period. 'Leading' is the term preferred by the NIV, and it better conveys what Ehud and Deborah and Gideon did, though they had a judicial function too. But we might question whether leading, let alone judging, was Samson's role. Yet the writer bookends this story of Samson's vulnerability and betrayal by Delilah with the words: 'Samson led Israel for twenty years.'[3] In 'the days of the Philistines' he did what was required of him. Without copying his moral failures, let us determine to follow his example of completing what God asks us individually to do.

Ponder what God has asked of you in the past. Have you been following his directions? Has pride led to your downfall? What will it involve for you to walk humbly with your God again?[4]

[1] Ps 119:1,2a, *The Message* [2] Cundall, pp173,174 [3] 15:20; 16:31b [4] Mic 6:8

A GOD OF REVERSALS

'God turns life around. Turned-around Jacob skips rope, turned-around Israel sings laughter.'[1] Praise with exuberance!

JUDGES 16:18–31

Samson's long locks were presumably only a symbol of his God-given strength. The greater tragedy of their cutting was not that he was deceived by his woman a second time but that, despite their connection to his Nazirite vow, 'he did not know that the LORD had left him' (v 20). The consequent pain and loss of sight were compounded by the shame of menial labour, his hands shackled at the grinding mill. Meanwhile, the captivity down in Gaza continues long enough for his hair to regrow – the significance of which escapes his captors' attention.

But he, and the Israel he represented (or, even better, the God he and the people worshipped) had the last laugh. The occasion of Samson's greatest Philistine slaughter is a festival in honour of their fertility god. As they celebrate Dagon, and with it the powerlessness of their nemesis, they chant, 'Our god has delivered our enemy into our hands' (v 24) – tribute to their god but also indirectly to Samson's impact on their nation. And when Samson pulls down their temple edifice, killing the leadership of the nation along with jeering spectators at the festival, Israel has every right to shout: 'Our God has delivered our enemy into our hands.'

For once, Samson prayed for God's direct intervention. Is this what made the difference? Or was it the climactic reversal that God had been planning for Samson for 20 years? Our God is a God of reversals, and many of the stories of Scripture turn on this theological tenet. Esther's success in saving her people, for example, turns on the discovery by the pagan king on a sleepless night of the value to his kingdom of her uncle Mordecai.[2] Daniel's survival in the lion's den opens the way for his elevation to a position of influence.[3] Jacob the deceiver becomes Israel the patriarch.[4]

Do you have faith that God can reverse a situation in your life or church which seems intractable? Talk to him about it.

[1] Ps 53:6b, *The Message* [2] Esth 6:1,2 [3] Dan 6:19–23,28 [4] Gen 32:28; Hos 12:3–6

LEADERSHIP VACUUM

'Good leadership is a channel of water controlled by GoD; he directs it to whatever ends he chooses.'[1] Thank God for good leaders in your life.

JUDGES 17

Judges closes with some profoundly disturbing stories, thematic rather than chronological appendices to the main narrative. They illustrate the problems of these dislocated times, corresponding (in Hebrew thematic balance) to the opening of the book (1:1 - 3:6). God is not mentioned (except in 20:18–28), no outside threat presents itself, and no judge is raised up. But though superficially things are moving along quietly (chs 17,18), underneath evil is fermenting (chs 19,21) and we see something of life among powerless people in the vacuum of leadership evident between Joshua and David.[2] With little editorial comment, the history is nevertheless recorded for Israel's instruction – and ours.[3]

Today's reading is richly revealing of the times, as a young Levite goes looking for work in the hill country of Ephraim. It was accepted that a blessing uttered by the originator of a curse could overcome the evil implied, though Micah's mother seems to be more into manipulation than cursing. (One wonders what happened to the other four-fifths of the money she got back from her son.) The carved image (v 3) was possibly a 'bull' intended to be the place for God to 'stand'. Was this also Aaron's intention at Sinai?[4] The consequences of his ancestor's action were either unknown to Micah or not sufficient warning. In any case, the bull, a frequent symbol for Baal in the Canaanite fertility cult, was an unfortunate choice for a follower of God.

A picture emerges of morally lost times, a Levite city system no longer within reach of all the tribes,[5] and disruption of ordinary family and community life. We do well to ponder the effects in our own society of a leadership vacuum and disregard of God's laws, especially in societies no longer subscribing to Christian values.

If you or someone close to you has the gift of leadership,[6] is it being used wisely and well?

[1] Prov 21:1, *The Message* [2] *See* Rom 15:4 [3] *See* 17:6; 18:1; 19:1; 21:25
[4] Exod 32 [5] Num 35:1–8; Josh 21:41,42 [6] Rom 12:7,8

A PRIEST FOR HIRE

'Teach me from your textbook on life. I'm your servant – help me understand what that means, the inner meaning of your instructions.'[1]

The Danites were in a particularly difficult situation.[2] They could not occupy the portion assigned to them[3] and were losing ground to the Amorites and Philistines. They had only a small area of hill country left and even on that (v 1b) they could not settle: the word 'camp' (v 12) implies temporary status. So the possibility of moving north 100 miles is canvassed. This time[4] the spies give a persuasive report, and apparently the whole decimated tribe (perhaps 3,000 people) moves.

When they enquired of the Lord (v 5), Micah's priest had a ready answer. Was it from God? Was he the kind of person to deliver, faithfully, a word so profoundly affecting their future? Though shrines were set up at different times and places throughout Israel before the temple was established in Jerusalem, they were usually associated with a theophany or special revelation,[5] but Micah's house is a domestication of God. Household 'gods' were generally frowned on, with any graven image expressly forbidden. Though the wandering Levite was to be preferred to Micah's own son (17:5,10), this was still outside the instructions God had given through Moses, but in a time of no leadership (v 1), any leadership seems better than none.

Whether we find our vocation in 'Christian ministry' or serve God as agents in his world, knowing and doing what God requires of us in the proper manner is paramount. Do we admire Micah for his enterprise? He started by stealing from his own mother. Does she give generously to honour God? Actually, she holds back most of the money. Is the Levite showing initiative in seeking work? He is a priest for hire. As we look beneath the surface in these stories, we find that doing right as we see fit (17:6) is not enough. Discerning through God's Spirit is essential.

A prayer: Lord, teach us to do your work in your way.

[1] Ps 119:124b,125, *The Message* [2] *See also* 1:34,35 [3] Josh 19:40–48 [4] *Cf* Num 13:31–33 [5] Exod 20:24

DANGER OF EXPEDIENCY

'Give me insight so I can do what you tell me – my whole life one long, obedient response. Guide me down the road.'[1]

JUDGES 18:14–31

Micah's priest was lured by opportunity for wider ministry (vs 19,20), though the threatening presence of 600 warriors perhaps also helped his decision! He shows no gratitude to his benefactor, and the practices he follows are doubtful, but there is enough in this example to warn us against easily leaving a place of faithful ministry for wider pastures so that we can influence more people for God. We must be careful that we do not make decisions for the sake of expediency, going against God's specific guidance, or running ahead before he has spoken.

The soldiers use an argument often at odds with Yahweh's strategy taught in Judges. 'Might is right; we are stronger than you' was proved wrong in the case of prophet/judge Deborah's encounter with the advanced technology of the invading chariot force of Sisera.[2] Judge Gideon was specifically instructed to reduce the number of his combatants to make it clear victory rested with God alone.[3] 'Might is right' also did not justify the treatment of Micah (vs 22–26), though his previous behaviour does not encourage us to feel sorry for him!

Nevertheless, the settling of the Dan tribe with its necessary elimination of the original inhabitants of their northern valley is in line with God's command to inhabit the whole land.[4] It is not condemned, nor is it implied that it is a consequence of the disorder and irregularity of life at the time. However, the establishment of a shrine complete with graven image was clearly wrong. Dan (and Bethel) later became alternative cult centres for a debased priesthood in the time of Jeroboam and a thorn in the side of the legitimate priests centred in Judah. How easily actions taken for what seem reasonable, or at least excusable, reasons become temptations to depart from God's clear instructions. How we need divine guidance!

When it is time to change vocation or place of service, what principles inform your listening for God's guidance?

[1] Ps 119:34,35a, *The Message* [2] Judg 4 [3] Judg 6 [4] Josh 1:1–5

WHAT HOSPITALITY IS THIS?

Celebrate God's hospitality: 'You'll welcome us with open arms when we run for cover to you. Let the party last all night!'[1]

These next few chapters describe events from an earlier period, when Bethel was the centre of religious activity. The penalty for adultery was death, so presumably the amicable meeting of the husband and father, and the extra donkey brought to take the woman home, favours the RSV translation of her behaviour – angry, not unfaithful (v 2). The lengthy stay at her father's house changed from eastern hospitality to delaying tactics, but the point of the story (v 12) is that Israelite hospitality should be safer than that of an alien city. But it wasn't, not even for a Levite. One wonders if, with such attitudes to women (v 24), a concubine could experience true hospitality anywhere.[2]

The story is well told. You sense the looming threat of a night in the square. Only an outsider offers hospitality – even though the Levite, having come well prepared, was not asking for the expected courtesies. However, a safe night is the very thing the man could not offer, even with bribes of women offered to the sexually charged men throwing themselves against the door. And so Gibeah becomes a byword for depravity,[3] though it was later the capital of King Saul.[4]

We shudder at the uncaring behaviour of the Levite who showed only anger when his 'possession' was killed. Dismembering and sending her body in 12 pieces suggests a ritual summons, with the story told in each tribe by the bearer of the grisly body part.[5] Several values of Israel are highlighted here in observance or breach: hospitality ranks highly, national obligation and unity of the tribes is also crucial. But protection of the powerless, especially women, carries little weight. Jesus returned the status of women to that intended at creation.[6] In the new covenant, baptism, a sign inclusive of all believers,[7] replaces circumcision. Thank God!

How hospitable are you and your church to strangers and foreigners in need?

[1] Ps 5:11a, *The Message* [2] *Cf* Gen 19:8 [3] Hos 9:9; 10:9 [4] 1 Sam 10:26; 15:34
[5] *Cf* 1 Sam 11:7 [6] Gen 1:26–28 [7] Gal 3:26–29

NOT A PRETTY OUTCOME

Meditate on the psalmist's affirmation: 'I know that you, GOD, are on the side of victims, that you care for the rights of the poor.'[1]

JUDGES 20

In recent years my congregation has sheltered victims of ethnic violence, including some who have suffered rape outside and inside refugee camps. I know other women too who would welcome public acknowledgement of the violence they have suffered, though rapists usually use fear to keep their victims silent. There are also women who have supported survivors of rape with organisations named after Tamar who, despite her horrific treatment by the men in her life, is listed with honour alongside Rahab and Uriah's wife in the forebears of Jesus.[2] Not many women, however, would seek vindication at the expense of being cut into 12 pieces at their death!

In fact there is little comfort in this story for any female victims, because the cause for which the tribes go to war (and the residents of Gibeah lose their lives) is the disregard of Israel's more 'core' values of hospitality and national solidarity, not the treatment of the woman.[3] These are the core values Benjamin is violating, and one last effort is made to bring solidarity before the renowned fighters of Judah, neighbours familiar with the area, begin the struggle against them. Despite their lesser numbers, the advantage is with the defenders until, on the third encounter, they are lured out from their hilly terrain. The principle at stake is that the future survival of the whole nation is more important than the fate of individual soldiers or even a whole tribe. Yet we must not consider normative the actions that accompany the Israelites' outrage. A 'just war' ethic argues that force must be commensurate with the threat and no more, but this fighting, begun by the Levite's less than full disclosure of his role in the treatment of his concubine (v 5) and exacerbated by some foolish vows, is out of all proportion to the offence. Food for thought as we consider recent international conflicts?

Lord, teach me your perspective on the evil around me and cause me to act courageously and justly.

[1] Ps 140:12, *The Message* [2] Gen 38; Matt 1:3 [3] Judg 19:23–26

A WAY FORWARD

'GOD, do it again – bring rains to our drought-stricken lives so those who planted their crops in despair will shout hurrahs at the harvest.'[1]

JUDGES 21

In the coming together of all Israel after the fighting (20:1), the parallels with Judges 1 and 2 are obvious. But now the battle is within the nation rather than without, as they face the consequences of their own rash promises and actions. Should the important values of hospitality and national solidarity really look like this? Does any action justify remedies like this? How often do our family or church feuds lose all sense of proportion about their core cause or desired outcome? Rules of order in worship or fellowship may sound good in theory, but in practice they may have an undesirable, even opposite, effect to that planned. It takes godly courage to put the spotlight on unintended outcomes, call a halt, and prayerfully seek God's wisdom to find a way through such dilemmas.

Of course, as later events show, a king (v 25) would not prevent disasters arising when God's subjects failed to consult him. But God does continue to redeem his people. The descendants of the tribe of Benjamin – the fruit of the Israelite 'rape of the Sabines'[2] marriage arrangements – eventually included Saul, Esther and the apostle Paul.[3] Finding a way through serious personal or community disputes, despite rash promises and actions, calls for creative insight and remedies – though not of the kind practised here! But we are promised that we only need to ask and God will give timely wisdom through his Spirit.[4] One home group in our church studying Hosea got tired of the constant descriptions of the waywardness of God's people and laid the book aside. But God, though his heart is grieving, does not turn aside from us – good news for all wandering sheep lacking shepherds. 'If we are faithless, he will remain faithful, for he cannot disown himself.'[5]

With the wisdom of hindsight, what actions have you taken that were foolish? Can you accept the forgiveness of the sovereign God and make a fresh start in his strength?

[1] Ps 126:4,5, *The Message* [2] Cundall, *Judges*, using the Roman historian Livy's story, p212 [3] 1 Sam 9:1; Esth 2:5–7; Rom 11:1 [4] James 1:5 [5] 2 Tim 2:13

RUTH

Ruth is a story of human loyalty. It relates to the period of the Judges and gives us insight into the domestic life of Israel at that time.

It is a tale of the friendship of Ruth (a Moabite woman) with her mother-in-law, Naomi. It is of special interest because it reminds us that King David was a descendant of Ruth and her husband, Boaz. On the human side, Jesus could trace his ancestry back through Ruth.[1] So the book of Ruth tells us that the messianic family, from which over a thousand years later the Messiah was born, included someone who was not a Jew.

The book of Ruth reminds us that God overrules in our lives. In due course Ruth was able to bring encouragement to Naomi, presenting her with a grandchild, Obed. That child in turn had a son named Jesse, who became the father of eight sons, one of whom was David.[2] God was working out his purpose in Ruth's circumstances even though she was not aware of it.

Outline
1 A story of love and loyalty	1:1 – 2:23
2 Ruth and Boaz	3:1 – 18
3 A wedding	4:1 – 22

---

[1] Matt 1:5,6 [2] Ruth 4:17

TRUE LOYALTY

Before reading today, deliberately call to mind the good things that God has done in your life in the past, and thank him for them.

After a brief account of family tragedy, we are quickly introduced to the widow Naomi whose horizon is filled with the bitterness of her loss, believing that she has little more to expect from life because her troubles have been brought about by a God who has 'afflicted' her (v 21).[1] In stark contrast, the young Moabite widow Ruth resolutely offers her mother-in-law loyal friendship that transcends the generational and racial gap between them. She is later aptly described by Boaz as one who has 'come to take refuge' under the wings of the God of Israel.[2]

Ruth has much to teach us about commitment in relationships. In an age where friends are often described as 'the new family', Ruth demonstrates that true friendship overcomes both personal background and difficult circumstances. Friendship is about more than feelings; it can be very costly, and yet infinitely rewarding. Naomi doesn't totally lose her grasp on the goodness of God, despite her heartache. She believes that God has come to the aid of his people (vs 6,7) and consequently instinctively wants to be in that place too. Part of the spirituality of the men and women of faith of Naomi's day was to deliberately remember the great acts of God in the past,[3] and we catch a glimpse here of that same resolve in Naomi.

While set in a vastly different context from twenty-first-century Western life, here nonetheless is the very stuff of contemporary human existence! We too live in turbulent, unpredictable times with war threatening to break out, widespread famine, refugees crossing national borders looking for security, and the deep pain of personal bereavement. Questions now, as then, about where God is in all this can in part be answered by recalling his past actions, which remind us of what he is like, and by encountering his love through others.

Pray for those you know struggling with tough circumstances or big questions about God, and ask God to help you be a good friend to them.

[1] Cf vs 13,20 [2] 2:12 [3] David Atkinson, *The Message of Ruth*, BST; IVP, 1983; Ps 77:3,11; Jonah 2:7

KINDNESS AND GENEROSITY

Slowly read 1 Peter 2:9–10 out loud. Prayerfully reflect on the contrasts, and praise God for his overwhelming kindness to you...

RUTH 2

Although Ruth was a young woman from a foreign country, in a culture where male protection was deemed a necessity, without hesitation she takes the initiative, placing herself in a vulnerable position to find a way to provide for Naomi and herself. Her courage and determination shine through again, so much so that she finds later that her reputation has gone before her (vs 10-12; 3:11). At harvest time the men would cut the grain, and the servant women follow behind binding it into sheaves. Moses' law required farmers to leave what the harvesters missed, so that the disadvantaged people of their day (the poor, widows, foreigners or fatherless) could gather food for themselves.[1]

Already the theme of emptiness in the first chapter – seen in famine, death, barrenness and hopelessness[2] – is beginning to be transformed. Harvest speaks of fullness. Boaz enters the story bringing compassion and generosity, and ultimately love and redemption. A wealthy older man, and a relative of Naomi's late husband, it is no accident that Ruth ends up gleaning the edges of his fields. Throughout this very human story God's hand can be seen. Verse 3 contains a rare Hebrew expression pointing to the truth that people ultimately do not control events because God is working his purposes out.[3]

At this stage, both are unaware of their future together. Ruth is preoccupied with Boaz's kindness to her as a foreigner, while Boaz, in simply choosing to obey God's law, opens the door to a realm of new possibilities. His obedience in helping the disadvantaged people of his day to help themselves was to lead to untold blessing in his own life.[4] Sensational headlines about asylum seekers can shape our attitudes but how would the God of Boaz want us to respond?

Find out more about what God thinks about asylum seekers by doing a Bible study on the word 'alien'. Encourage your church or home group to think and pray about this issue.

[1] *See* Lev 19:9; 23:22; Deut 24:19 [2] L Ryken, *Words of Delight: A Literary Introduction to the Bible*, Baker, 1987 [3] Cundall, p270 [4] *Cf* Isa 58:6–11

GODLY CHARACTER

'Go before us in our pilgrimage of life. Anticipate our needs, prevent our falling, and lead us into our destiny. Thank you, Lord. Amen.'[1]

The dramatic climax of the story approaches, as Ruth is coached by her mother-in-law in how to approach Boaz. If things worked out well, they would be rescued from poverty and Ruth would have a husband. As her dead husband's heir, Boaz had the right as kinsman redeemer to marry her under the dowry already paid by her deceased husband.[2] To us, Ruth's behaviour may sound provocative and risky, but her integrity is never in question. Her confidence is in Boaz as next of kin, and selflessly she makes herself vulnerable so that the family line can be continued through marriage. Interestingly, Ruth ignores one of Naomi's instructions and takes the initiative in overtly asking Boaz to make a symbolic claim to marriage by placing his garment over her. In so doing, he echoes the blessing from God that he had spoken over her earlier, and follows what remains today an Arab custom.[3] Here is a woman who again risks all for love, reminding us that we don't have to be powerful or influential to be effective as Christians – just purposeful in loving God and others.[4]

Boaz is described as a man of standing (2:1); his name means 'in him is strength'. In a relatively lawless era he chose to live up to his name. He could easily have dodged his responsibilities because there was actually another candidate for the role. However, he responds warmly and generously, keen to protect Ruth's honour and to do all he can.

Here are two people who with humility, perseverance, generosity and kindness are intentional about how they live their lives before God. In so doing they point to what God himself is like and, forward down through the centuries, to Jesus himself.[5] Our workplaces, neighbourhoods and churches also desperately need people of character living intentionally as apprentices of Jesus, with lives pointing towards him.

What would you like as your epitaph? How would you like others to describe your character? Ask the Holy Spirit for help in bridging the gap!

[1] Ray Simpson, *Celtic Daily Light*, Hodder & Stoughton, 1997 [2] Deut 25; Gen 38
[3] *See also* Ezek 16:8 [4] 1 Cor 1:26–30 [5] Rom 5:1–8

BIG PICTURE STUFF!

'Yet I will rejoice in the Lord ... The Sovereign Lord is my strength; he makes my feet like the feet of a deer, he enables me to tread on the heights.'[1]

RUTH 4

This chapter starts with Boaz at the city gate, the central place for debate and justice, in a complicated negotiation over some land that is part of the kinsman-redeemer arrangement. We aren't told the details of the relationship between the land sale and Ruth's marriage, nor do we know how Naomi acquired it in the first place. We only know that how the nearer relative responds will determine the whole outcome. Motivated by his love for Ruth and his willingness to give his money for her sake and that of the family name, Boaz succeeds in persuading the nearer kinsman to offer the right of redemption to him.

The story concludes with marriage, a son and heir, and an end to Naomi's emptiness as she cradles the living expression of God's blessing on her life. In her anguish she could not have imagined that things would turn out this way – but God had never let her go. In the darkest times in our lives he will not let us go either. This story exemplifies the truth that he shapes our circumstances and moulds us in them for our good.[2] Are you under significant work pressure? Or maybe you're in church leadership and things seem to be going nowhere? How can you allow God to shape you in the midst of it all?

The concluding genealogy at first appears as an inappropriately boring end to this beautiful story. In fact it is a 'literary device to make the transition from a microscopic examination of how God works in an out-of-the-way place among out-of-the-way people to telescopic vision of the immense reaches of God's ways'.[3] This is big-picture stuff: the story of Ruth is a single part in the epic narration of cosmic salvation! In the same way we need to see our lives and our churches as also a part of that cosmic story!

Pray for those who lead local churches. While seeming OK in public, church leaders can often be in a pressured lonely place, especially if their church isn't obviously flourishing.

[1] Hab 3:18,19 [2] Rom 8:28; Jer 29:11 [3] EH Peterson, *Five Smooth Stones for Pastoral Work*, Knox, 1986, p106

1 SAMUEL

1 Samuel is about three great characters whose lives overlapped: Samuel, Saul and David. The account is not complete, but for ancient authors, what an event meant was more important than its exact timing. 1 Samuel is more than simple history; it is the story of God's dealings with his people.

The book of Judges concluded by telling us that anarchy prevailed in Israel because 'Israel had no king'.[1] Although Samuel, the last judge, was popular, his influence was local and limited. The people wanted a national leader. Their request for a king was not just a criticism of Samuel; it was a rejection of God's leadership.[2] They wanted a king to be like the pagan nations around them. Samuel warned them that while kings may have potential for good, they also have potential for evil, as God's people would learn.[3]

King Saul began well. However, we can follow his gradual deterioration as he began to take matters into his own hands, making rash vows and disobeying God's commands. As God's replacement for Saul, David was a man whose faith was great. It was King David who finally dealt with the Philistines, the troublesome enemies of Israel.

Specially gifted by the Spirit for his work – God called him 'a man after my own heart'[4] – David was to become a great leader, Israel's greatest king and ancestor of the Messiah – Jesus, 'the Son of David'.

Outline

1 Eli and Samuel	1:1 – 7:17
2 Samuel and Saul	8:1 – 15:35
3 Saul and David	16:1 – 31:13

---

[1] Judg 21:25 [2] 1 Sam 8:7 [3] 1 Sam 8:10–18 [4] 1 Sam 13:14; Acts 13:22

PAIN, PRAYER, PROMISE

'He has remembered his love and his faithfulness to the house of Israel; all the ends of the earth have seen the salvation of our God.'[1]

1 SAMUEL 1

The history of Israel's monarchy stretches over the four books of Samuel and Kings. However, it begins not with a triumphant introduction to the first king but with a deeply troubled woman. Hannah had married a man who served God faithfully and who loved her in spite of her childlessness. But the 'in spite of' is significant. Childlessness was an unbearable stigma. If, as seems likely, Elkanah married Peninnah precisely because Hannah was childless, then his 'don't I mean more to you than ten sons' (v 8) must have rubbed salt in the wound – she clearly did not mean that to him! Peninnah's taunting, probably reflecting her own unhappiness, added to Hannah's misery.

Presumably Hannah prayed every year, but this year it was on a different scale. In spite of Eli's initial pastoral insensitivity (v 14), she found real peace (v 18). Whether or not she saw Eli's words as a promise from God, this year God 'remembered' Hannah and at last she conceived and Samuel was born (vs 19,20). Hannah's vow (v 22) may seem horrific, but children then were weaned much later and we must read the passage within its own cultural context. The final note that he 'worshipped the LORD there' is perhaps included to reassure readers that Samuel was OK! Was Hannah's vow trying to twist God's arm or expressing a long-held desire to dedicate a son to God? The writer doesn't ask; what mattered to him was that, having made a vow, she kept it. We too need to keep any promises we make to God.

One of the surprising things about the writer (almost certainly a man) here is his understanding of his own culture and his perceptive presentation not only of Elkanah's obtuseness and Eli's bumbling but also of the women's perspective and pain. This sense that God really does understand where we are coming from is very important.

Do you see yourself as more like Elkanah, Eli, Hannah or Penninah? Give thanks that God understands you.

[1] Ps 98:3

UPS AND DOWNS

'Who is God besides the LORD? And who is the Rock except our God? It is God who arms me with strength and keeps my way secure.'[1]

1 SAMUEL 2:1–11

Try reading through this prayer twice, first as Hannah's reflection on and response to her own circumstances and then as a theological introduction to the history of kingship in Israel. It works very well in both contexts, and the writer almost certainly intends it to be viewed both ways. It matters that we recognise the relevance of God's holiness, uniqueness and sovereignty both in individual daily living and on the world stage, in national and international politics. It should affect our attitude to shopping and to policy on Iraq. Hannah knew from her own experience that God's perspective is different from ours, that circumstances can be transformed, that God makes the weak strong and the strong weak, that pride is a danger, and that it is not human power that counts for anything but God's will.

Samuel and Kings spend much time discussing who is in charge, who is the most important, who has the most power, but the whole, often less than glorious, story has to be read in the context of this prayer. Leadership was never meant to be about pride and power, but about recognising God and helping his people, his faithful servants (v 9), to live in his way. The fact that God can and will turn human values and human ideas of status and power upside down is a great encouragement to those who see themselves as weak and struggling, but also a great challenge to those who view themselves as powerful. All God's people need to know that 'it is not by strength that one prevails' (v 9).

It is significant that this is recorded as Hannah's prayer. Reflecting on what God's character and presence mean for our individual lives and circumstances is a responsibility for all – not one meant to be handed over to the professional clergy or theologians.

Lord God, who knows our hearts, weighs deeds and transforms circumstances, help me to think through and live out the implications of what I see of you at work in my life.

---

1 2 Sam 22:32,33

LIGHT IN DARKNESS

'You, Lord, keep my lamp burning; my God turns my darkness into light.'[1]

1 SAMUEL 2:12–36

This section reads like a double-layered sandwich! The innocent goodness and growth of the young Samuel is interwoven with the awfulness of Eli's sons. They 'had no regard for the Lord' (v 12). In theory, they served God and his people, but in practice they served no one but themselves. For them, God, if he existed, was completely irrelevant in terms of everyday life, and the point of offerings was to replenish their own supplies. The people's desires were as irrelevant as God's. The crime was not so much the change of practice – the three-pronged fork is not mentioned in the ritual law – but that they treated 'the Lord's offering with contempt' (v 17). We are told that they were immoral and arrogant as well as irreligious. Eli's feeble remonstrances were swept aside. The relevance of Hannah's prayer is clear. As anyone hearing or heeding that would know, 'those who oppose the Lord will be broken' (v 10). Verse 25 confirms this as part of Scripture's ongoing reflection on the relationship between God's sovereignty and human responsibility.[2] It does not imply that the sons were not responsible. Today, too, Christian leaders face stricter judgement than others.[3]

And in the midst of this evil, corruption and defiance, Samuel 'grew up in the presence of the Lord' (v 21) and 'in favour with the Lord and with people' (v 26). What a tribute to old Eli! There is a real challenge here for us not to write off as 'dead' churches where we can clearly see corruption or irreligion or to assume that God cannot be working there. It may be that even in those places there are those who are growing up in the presence of the Lord.

Unexpectedly, Eli is condemned as well as his sons. He rebuked his sons, but he also ate from their wrongly obtained offerings. Those 'given much' are held particularly responsible.[4]

Pray for those who are growing up in the presence of corruption and violence, that they might also know the presence of the Lord.

[1] Ps 18:28 [2] Cf eg, Acts 2:23 [3] James 3:1; cf Mal 2:7–9 [4] Luke 12:48

WHO SAID THAT?

'Listen, you heavens, and I will speak; hear, you earth, the words of my mouth. Let my teaching fall like rain and my words descend like dew.'[1]

1 SAMUEL 3:1 – 4:1a

How good are you at listening? I find it very easy, particularly chatting with friends on the phone, to let my attention be diverted. I'm still hearing their words, but if I've switched on to something else I'm no longer really listening. Eli's attention had been diverted by the (oh, so delicious) food that his sons prepared from the illicit offerings.[2] God had to get his attention another way.

Sometimes it is possible to be listening so hard for an expected ring on the doorbell that we don't realise that actually, the phone is ringing! Samuel was certainly listening. He was expecting to hear Eli, who often needed help in the night. So when the sound came he was absolutely sure Eli was calling. It was perhaps easier to think old Eli was confused than to recognise that this call really was different.

It is ironic that it was Eli himself who eventually enabled Samuel to tune in to God's words and therefore hear the terrible message of judgement on his household. We learn a lot here about both characters. Samuel was clearly a kind, willing worker – he got up three times without complaint – and sensitive enough to want to avoid delivering the hard message. Eli was clearly a good teacher and mentor. He wanted to hear from God, even if it was a hard message to deliver and to hear. He was humble enough to let God speak to him through a child.

We might see this message of judgement as unsuitable for children, but God trusted Samuel not only to hear it but also to deliver it to Eli. Do we sometimes try so hard to protect children that we prevent them from hearing from God or speaking for God? This was the (necessary?) beginning of a great ministry for Samuel (4:1a).

What distractions or predetermined expectations might prevent me from hearing God if he speaks in an unexpected way? Would I be as willing as Eli to listen to a child?

---

[1] Deut 32:1 [2] 1 Sam 2:29

FATAL CONSEQUENCES

'Who is this King of glory? The Lord strong and mighty, the Lord mighty in battle ... The Lord Almighty – he is the King of glory.'[1]

1 SAMUEL 4:1b–11

Years ago I overheard two 11-year-olds arguing. I can't remember what it was about but I remember well the clinching argument: 'Well our house has got a back-boiler and yours hasn't'! This passage also reflects the 'my dad is bigger than your dad' syndrome. Israel thought that they could use the Ark of God as a talisman; it would be the clinching argument in their fight with Philistia. The Philistines were afraid, for they did recognise the power of Israel's God, but the presence of the Ark had the opposite result to the one the Israelites had intended. Rather than causing the Philistines to give in without a fight, it stimulated them to fight even harder and the Israelite army was crushed.

This was not the only time that Israel put superstitious trust in the symbols of religion and failed to recognise that the symbol is of no value without an understanding of the reality behind it. In Jeremiah's time they thought that because they possessed 'the temple of the Lord' they were invulnerable,[2] and many prophets were accused of lack of faith because they prophesied the destruction of Jerusalem, seen as God's own city and therefore again, invulnerable.[3] But Israel's God is not an idol or a Baal. He cannot be manipulated to ensure personal gain. Israel had forgotten that the Ark represented 'The Lord's covenant'. They had set aside relationship with God and failed to serve or obey him, yet they still thought that the presence of the Ark would ensure victory.

For today's Christians, wearing a cross round the neck or a 'what would Jesus do' bracelet, attending church services or even exhibiting all kinds of external 'spiritual gifts' are only meaningful if they reflect a living, loving and serving relationship with God and with others.[4]

Lord, forgive us for trusting the trappings of religion rather than you, and help us to take seriously our own responsibility to serve and to love.

[1] Ps 24:8,10 [2] Jer 7:4 [3] eg Mic 2:6; 3:8–12 [4] Cf 1 Cor 13:4–7

THE LIGHT HAS GONE OUT

'Though the fig-tree does not bud and there are no grapes on the vines, though ... the fields produce no food ... yet ... I will be joyful in God my Saviour.'[1]

1 SAMUEL 4:12–22

Sometimes something happens which makes us feel life will never be the same again: the death of President Kennedy or Princess Diana, the closure of a factory which means a town will die, the fire which destroys a priceless library. For Eli the loss of the Ark, even when he had half-expected it, was a devastating shock, more so even than the defeat of the army or the death of his sons. The shock caused him to fall but it is somewhat ironic that what actually killed him was the broken neck caused by his excess weight – perhaps stemming from all the special food taken from the people's offerings to God.[2]

His daughter-in-law was equally upset. The loss of the Ark and the deaths of Eli and her husband Phineas were apparently as much responsible for her death as the problems with her labour. Her friends tried to ease her dying moments by reminding her that her son's birth brought meaning to her own suffering. But how could she find any comfort at his birth when she was leaving him in a nation where God no longer lived? Giving him the dreadful name 'No Glory' reflected her own despair. He was unlikely to find any happiness or even survive in an Israel without God. Wrong theology has far-reaching consequences and, as we shall see, hers was definitely wrong! Her dedication to God and her belief that without his presence disaster is inevitable was praiseworthy. But she assumed that when the symbols of God's presence are removed then God himself could no longer be active. How often have we heard believers despairing because Christian symbols have been removed from public view? Are we tempted to think that Jesus is any less present because nativity scenes are not permitted in the shopping centre? We are equally wrong!

Lord, help us get the balance right between caring about your visible presence in our world and yet not despairing if only the invisible remains.

[1] Hab 3:17,18 [2] 1 Sam 2:29

OR HAS IT?

'I will show the holiness of my great name, which has been profaned among the nations ... Then the nations will know that I am the LORD.'[1]

1 SAMUEL 5

One sometimes feels that Christians are a little afraid of humour, as if laughter and the things of God should somehow be kept apart. The writers of Scripture do not share the same scruples! The comedy in this chapter is rather dark but it is definitely there. One can imagine later Israelites falling about when this story was read. The theology of the Philistines was even more wrong than that of the Israelites. Psalm 2:4 makes it clear that attempts to oppose God can only be seen as laughable. The Philistines were convinced that because they had defeated the Israelite army, captured the Ark of God and placed it in the temple of their god Dagon, this proved Dagon's superiority over Israel's God. How wrong could they be? The Lord is Sovereign over the whole world. The defeat of a disbelieving and disobedient Israel was an expression, not a contradiction, of that sovereignty. The events of this chapter indicate this, and provide further lessons for both Israel and Philistia.

It is important for believers today to get their theology right and to know enough about their faith to be able to speak up for their beliefs. However, sometimes Christians are clearly defeated in argument by atheistic philosophers or scientists. When this happens it is tempting for those on both sides to conclude that God himself has now been defeated and can no longer be seen as active or even existent. The god of reason and human intellect has triumphed! But don't be deceived. This chapter encourages us to think again. It may be that we have been defeated because of our own over-confidence, wrong theology or misplaced trust. But whether or not this is so, remember that God is quite capable of defending himself without our help, and that eventually even modern Philistines will have to recognise his presence and his power!

Help me, Sovereign Lord, to realise that if I am defeated it does not mean you are defeated.

[1] Ezek 36:23

DEALING WITH FALLOUT

'Who among the gods is like you, LORD? Who is like you – majestic in holiness, awesome in glory, working wonders?'[1]

1 SAMUEL 6:1 – 7:1

Scepticism is not a modern phenomenon! How much evidence is needed before we accept that the spread of AIDS is largely linked to inappropriate and unwise sexual behaviour, or that excessive use of carbon-based energy really will cause climate change? The Philistines were faced with overwhelming evidence of God's activity among them, but of course it could all have been coincidence. Their problem therefore was how to return the Ark in a way that placated Israel's God, if indeed it was he who had caused all their troubles, but did not give an unnecessary advantage to Israel, if in fact it had all been coincidence. They solved it by sending a cart pulled by cows still within earshot of their newborn calves. Ingenious! One wonders whether the Philistine sceptics were convinced when the cows headed straight for Israel rather than back towards their calves!

But the saddest part of this story is not the scepticism of the Philistines but the reaction of the Israelites from Beth Shemesh who received the Ark. In spite of everything that had happened, they seemed less aware of the power and holiness of their God than most of the Philistines had become. Their first thought was not to worship God but to check out what riches the Philistines might have sent back inside the Ark, given the extent of the gold sent with it. It seems they were more in awe of gold than they were of God. Their presumption was punished as heavily as that of their enemies.

Sometimes our desire to make clear the loving, gracious nature of our God leads us to forget the awesome nature of his holiness. It is easier to forget about uncomfortable passages like this one. CS Lewis catches the point when he reminds us that Aslan is not a tame lion.[2]

Lord, sometimes I, too, find it hard to see you in the continuing coincidences, and sometimes I, too, am more impressed by gold than by your holiness. Please forgive me.

---

[1] Exod 15:11 [2] In *The Lion, the Witch and the Wardrobe*

A LIFETIME OF SERVICE

'Lead me to the rock that is higher than I. For you have been my refuge, a strong tower against the foe.'[1]

1 SAMUEL 7:2–17

I remember Miss Brewer. She was an old lady who led the young people's work at our church when I was 12 or 13. When new younger couples arrived and took over we hardly noticed that she had gone but she dropped out, without a hint of resentment, having prepared the way and made sure a whole generation understood what it meant to love and to serve Jesus.

Samuel is usually remembered for his early childhood and for his later years when he handed over first to Saul and then to David. But in between were many years of effective ministry. This chapter tells us just how much the Israelites owed him. He travelled the land explaining what it meant to love the Lord. He showed them that serving God meant much more than just paying lip service but involved total commitment in every area of life. He administered justice, gave them a sense of purpose and prayed for them. He understood the usefulness of visual and verbal aids and set up the Ebenezer 'stone of help' to act as a constant reminder of what God had done for them in the past and therefore to help keep them on the right path in the future. It may be that the beginning and the end of Samuel's life had special significance, but we should not underestimate the significance of the years of faithful service that lay between the two.

Miss Brewer would never have seen herself as a significant leader, never have put herself forward and certainly never have compared herself to Samuel. But in many ways she did for us what Samuel did for Israel. Samuel is portrayed, not as a hero that we could never imitate, but as an example of a faithful, godly, servant finding ways of helping others serve God.

Give thanks for those whose faithful service helped you understand God's path for you. Is there anyone you could remind that 'thus far the LORD has helped' (v 12)?

[1] Ps 61:2,3

MIXED MOTIVES

'Examine me, God, and know my mind; test me and understand my anxious thoughts ... and lead me in the everlasting way.'[1]

Samuel had grown up very much aware of the problems caused by the corruption of Eli's sons, but he had clearly not learned from Eli's mistakes. It was primarily his decision to appoint his own corrupt sons as leaders that caused the tribal elders to request a king. It is hard to be objective about the gifts and faults of those we love, but it remains vital for the well-being of God's people that nepotism is avoided in the appointment of leaders. The elders (vs 4,5) are often portrayed in an entirely negative way, but the words they use are part of God's pattern for kingship found in Deuteronomy 17:14 and it seems likely that one reason for their request was their desire that the nation continue to follow God in the way that Samuel had taught them. His sons would certainly not help them in that, and a king just might.

God is aware that their motives are mixed, and that their request also reflects a lack of trust in him and an over dependence on the strategies used by other nations. Nevertheless, after making sure that they are warned about the negative consequences of the appointment of a king he tells Samuel to grant their request. This was to be the way in which God would work with Israel in the future.

Sometimes when new strategies are proposed in a church it is easy for older folk, like Samuel, to see all the negatives, to be upset that their ideas are being replaced and perhaps to ignore their mistakes which led to the new proposals in the first place. They may even be right about the negative consequences! But in the end Samuel recognised that this was God's way forward and put his energies into facilitating the change. Do we have the courage to do the same?

Lord, we know that most human systems have both negative and positive effects. Help us work with you in maximising positive and minimising negative effects of systems in our church.

[1] Ps 139:23,24, REB

DISCOVERING POTENTIAL

'The LORD is trustworthy in all he promises and faithful in all he does. The LORD upholds all who fall and lifts up all who are bowed down.'[1]

1 SAMUEL 9:1 – 10:8

Saul, tall and handsome, might have looked like a king but in most other ways he seems an unlikely candidate. He had little religious awareness, he lacked confidence and his servant seems to have had a lot more initiative than he had. But this was the man chosen by God to be ruler, deliverer and governor of God's own people. Samuel knew from the beginning that this was God's choice, so he spent time talking to him, eating with him and generally building up his confidence. Samuel knew that it was not this Saul who was called to be king, but rather the Saul who would emerge after his encounter with the Spirit of God on the way home, the 'different person'[2] that he would become. Nevertheless, it was this Saul whom Samuel anointed.

Over the years I have come across several students training for Christian ministry of one kind or another who sensed that they were called by God quite a while before they actually came to know him for themselves. Often it was the help, support, trust and general mentoring of older Christians that brought them through to faith and helped them to understand their own calling. Also over the years I have seen some very unlikely candidates (at least in my view!) emerge as those whom God has chosen to use in very significant ways. Again, often this happened when some other Christian recognised their potential and trusted them with significant responsibility before it was obvious to others that they would be able to carry it.

Like Samuel, these Christians, usually but not always older, were open to hearing from God about the potential for service present in unusual sources. They saw the 'different person' that could emerge after an encounter with God's Spirit. Can we?

Have you sensed that God has a special purpose for someone you know? If so, try praying for them, talking to them and trusting them. You never know what might emerge.

[1] Ps 145:13,14 [2] 1 Sam 10:6

MAKING AN APPOINTMENT

'Here is my servant ... my chosen one in whom I delight; I will put my Spirit on him, and he will bring justice to the nations.'[1]

1 SAMUEL 10:9–27

I have to confess that I get very frustrated when someone responds to the thanks of others for some particular ministry that they have found helpful by saying, 'It wasn't me, it was the Lord.' Of course, we understand what they mean, but one of the key interests of the Old Testament is the way in which God and human beings work together in the carrying out of God's purposes. We see something of that in this chapter.

The prophetic group provide a context for the Spirit once more to touch Saul. The neighbours recognise the change that God has brought about in Saul. His reticence in talking with his uncle perhaps teaches him that he still has more changing to do. The Lord ensures that all the people understand Saul to be his choice and not just Samuel's, but Samuel still plays a key role in working it all through. The 'rights and duties of kingship' (v 25) make it clear that all parties have responsibilities to carry out if this system is going to work for Israel. The valiant men, because God had touched their hearts (v 26), dedicate themselves to working with Saul, helping him to fulfil his God-given responsibilities. The 'scoundrels' (v 27) are those who refuse to recognise that Saul might have a part to play in the saving of God's people.

There was no way that Saul could fulfil his kingly duties without God's help, but that doesn't mean that his part was irrelevant. God chose to require the cooperation of both the king and the people to carry out his purposes for Israel. It seems that God enjoys working with people as well as for them. Surely God will be pleased rather than offended by the recognition that one of his servants has been instrumental in helping others.

Lord, help me to recognise you at work in my life and in the lives of others today, and to enjoy with you the fact that we can work together.

---

[1] Isa 42:1

SAUL IN HIS HEYDAY

'This is what the LORD says: "In the time of my favour I will answer you, and in the day of salvation I will help you."'[1]

1 SAMUEL 11

Most of us sometimes experience that wonderful feeling that says, 'Today I got it right'. And maybe once or twice in a lifetime we might even reach the stage of 'after what has happened today, even if I never achieve anything else, this makes it all worthwhile'. I think this was one of those days for Saul. He positively oozed kingship qualities! He saw what needed to be done and acted promptly, firmly and effectively. He didn't try to do it all on his own, but involved the whole nation. He gave full recognition to God's involvement in events; he was even able to act graciously to those who had previously refused to recognise his calling. The excessive violence on both sides perhaps seems offensive to modern believers but would not have been an issue in that context. For them, Saul was unquestionably a hero. He had been appointed as God's choice and now he was clearly also the people's choice. No wonder there was such a huge celebration (v 15)!

Without this chapter we may have wondered why it was that God chose Saul. The account of the rest of his life is largely a sad story of increasing failure and mental collapse, but here we see him fulfilling his potential, a picture of what he could have been if he had not been taken over by an obsession with holding on to power. It stands as both an encouragement and a warning to us. An encouragement, because it shows that unlikely people really can come through to do great things, and that with God's help and the total cooperation of the people apparently unassailable enemies can be defeated. A warning for us because, as for Saul and throughout history, success and public acclamation can very easily become addictive and the search for more and more approbation can very easily cause major problems.

Think about and rejoice in your successes. Thank God for them and pray that they will not lead you astray.

[1] Isa 49:8

SAMUEL'S MEMOIRS

'Look to the LORD and his strength; seek his face always. Remember the wonders he has done, his miracles, and the judgements he pronounced.'[1]

1 SAMUEL 12:1–15

Samuel had been in the job a long time. Although he continued in many duties within Israel, in effect this ceremony confirming Saul's kingship was also Samuel's retirement party. Any of us leaving a job we have loved, particularly where it involves handing over responsibility for a situation we still care deeply about, have very mixed feelings. We see this reflected in the final speeches of presidents and prime ministers or the last sermons of long-standing Christian ministers as well as in our own experience. Samuel was no different. He wanted to set an agenda for the future, but first takes the opportunity to look back, reviewing both his own life and that of the nation.

It mattered to Samuel that he left with a clean slate, that any problems be cleared up. The universal acknowledgement that he had done a good job and need have no regrets must have really encouraged him. He had in no way abused his power as a leader. I often think that if I am to be a cheerful, generous and warm-hearted old lady rather than a 'moany old bag' who constantly criticises and always sees the negatives in life, then I have to keep practising now! A retirement party like Samuel's, where everyone is able to give thanks for a lifetime of positive service and there are no regrets on any side, can only happen if, like Samuel, we have lived the life first. It's never too soon to work at becoming the people we want to be eventually!

The review of the nation's history is less positive. God has clearly fulfilled his part of the covenant – but the people equally obviously have not. Now they have a new chance. If king and people both played their part, then the nation could be transformed. Even if we can't look back on a job well done, we can still look forward with hope to a transformed future.

Thank you, God, for all you have done for me in the past. Help me live now in a way that will bring no regrets in the future.

[1] 1 Chr 16:11,12

SAMUEL'S LEGACY

'God is our refuge and strength, an ever-present help in trouble. Therefore we will not fear, though the earth give way ... The LORD Almighty is with us.'[1]

1 SAMUEL 12:16–25

It isn't always easy to be positive about a new initiative in the church when in your heart of hearts you feel a wrong decision has been made. Samuel faced the same dilemma. He wasn't happy about the monarchy and he couldn't stop himself making his feelings clear on that point. But when the people responded with a real sense of repentance for any wrong motivation, and perhaps were contemplating abandoning the new system, Samuel pulled himself together. He also knew in his heart of hearts that this was now God's way forward for the future. His job was not to criticise the system but to encourage them to carry it through in a way that would enable the nation to live in a way that honoured God and reflected their calling to live as God's covenant people. He wanted them to be constantly aware of the reality of that calling and that identity. He reassured them about God's continuing commitment to them and his own commitment to keep praying for them even after his retirement (vs 22,23). He challenged them to keep remembering what God had done for them in the past, to keep trusting God for the future, and to serve God with all their hearts in the present (vs 20,24).

In a constantly changing world like ours, it is not surprising that many people have reservations about new programmes or new patterns of doing things. It would be easy just to be critical and walk away from it all, but what the church needs is people like Samuel who can overcome their reservations: people who can recognise that even when a system is not perfect it can still be used by God, who can encourage those involved to apply the system in a way that honours God, and who will commit themselves to keep praying.

'Lord, forgive me for the times when personal reservations prevent me from recognising your continued involvement in changing systems. Help me to enable others make the new systems work well.'

[1] Ps 46:1,2,7

THE COST OF DISOBEDIENCE

Lord, still my heart to hear your voice.

New governments and leaders can lose their shine very quickly. The politician who seemed so attractive in the election campaign can soon be seen as a tyrant, or simply incompetent. Israel's new monarchy was no exception. God had allowed the people to have their way, yet in his grace he still held out the promise of success (12:13–15). Sadly, King Saul wasn't up to it, and a sorry chapter in his – and Israel's – story begins.

Whatever the truth about Saul's age and the length of his rule (the Hebrew text lacks the figures in verse 1 and the Greek text omits the verse completely, so versions which give numbers in verse 1 are usually trying to reconstruct the chronology), the direction of his reign was set early on, and it wasn't very encouraging. First, his attempt at decisiveness committed the Israelites to guerrilla war and thus a hopelessly small army (v 2). Jonathan's skirmish with the Philistines may have been successful initially, but it attracted the attention of the main army. No wonder the Israelites were afraid (vs 6,7). Then when his men began to drift off, tired of waiting for Samuel to arrive, Saul's impatience led to sin. He offered the sacrifice himself (v 9).

To his credit, when Samuel did eventually arrive, Saul told the truth. But perhaps in doing so he also exposed his naivety, not appearing to see any problem with what he had done (vs 11,12). Samuel's response must have seemed chilling (v 14). And yet there also seemed to be an element of mercy. This was not like Belshazzar's feast.[1] While Saul might not now start a dynasty, the kingdom was not to be taken away from him. God was looking further ahead; Saul's successor wasn't yet ready for the task.

'Only he who believes is obedient and only he who is obedient believes.'[2] To what acts of obedience is God calling you today?

[1] Dan 5:25–30 [2] Dietrich Bonhoeffer, *The Cost of Discipleship*, SCM, 1963

GETTING ON WITH THE JOB

'My goal is God himself, not joy, nor peace, nor even blessing, but Himself, my God.'[1]

1 SAMUEL 14:1–23

Israel was in a bad way. The army was down to 600 from 3,000 (v 2; *cf* 13:2). Some had escaped, others had gone into hiding (13:6,7) and Saul seemed to be paralysed into inactivity. Jonathan however, frustrated by doing nothing, decided run a secret operation (v 1). His plan seemed crazy to say the least. The only way to approach the Philistines was by climbing up a cliff. Even if they got there, Jonathan and his young armour bearer would be hopelessly outnumbered. But two things drove him: the Philistines were 'uncircumcised' (v 6; CEV has 'godless'); and if this was what God wanted, nothing could hinder him from saving them. Numbers were irrelevant (v 6). What kind of king might Jonathan have become had his father not sinned?

Like many before and since, Jonathan looked for a sign that God was with him. Acting in faith doesn't mean being foolhardy (vs 8–10). Sure enough, the sign came from the arrogant and overconfident Philistines (vs 11,12). Scaling a cliff before attacking and beating a much bigger enemy is usually the stuff of comic books. But here God was involved and that was what made the difference. The details of exactly how the two of them beat a force at least ten times their number are much less significant (v 14).

Jonathan's private enterprise was only the beginning. God was at work. Suddenly the whole Philistine army was affected and even Saul took notice (v 16). He seemed to start well and began to ask God what he should do (v 18) but then he realised that there wasn't time (v 19) and just got on with it. The apparently spiritual answer is not necessarily the godly one. When God is moving, sometimes we just have to act.

'I never worry about action, but only about inaction.'[2] Ask God to help you overcome inertia which stops you from doing his will.

---

1 F Brook **2** Winston Churchill, 1874–1965

LEADING OR LED?

'I'm thanking you, God, from a full heart, I'm writing the book on your wonders.'[1]

1 SAMUEL 14:24–52

The decisiveness so often expected in leaders can often be thinly disguised rashness. Saul tried to demonstrate his determination to complete the victory over the Philistines by insisting that his men fast until the evening (v 24). But what did he think it would achieve? They needed all the energy they could get! Even worse, despite the severity of his command, he failed to make sure that everyone knew about the curse (v 27). Everyone obeyed… apart from Jonathan.

Once again we have a glimpse of Jonathan's unfulfilled potential as a national leader. His practicality was uncomplicated. If the honey was there, why not eat it? Of course, if God had commanded them not to eat, it would have been a different matter. But Saul had made a rod for his own back by imposing on his men what God had not. It's a failing which has not gone away. One of the unpleasant side effects of religion is the desire to create unnecessary rules.[2] How can we be rigorous in examining our own traditions to ensure that they go no further in their demands than does God himself?

The fast which Saul imposed was for the daytime. By evening, his ravenous men could wait no longer. They killed the plundered animals right where they were. But that meant breaking a law which God actually had given.[3] Now Saul does his best to put it right by offering a practical solution (vs 33,34). Sadly, when it emerges that Jonathan has broken the fast, albeit unwittingly, Saul is unable to bring the same practical thinking to bear (v 44). It is left to his men, who had already protected Jonathan by remaining silent (v 39), to ensure his deliverance from the consequences of his father's rashness (v 45). Whether or not Saul could see it, they knew that God was behind the day's victory.

Leaders are not infallible. Do you know of leaders who need wise advice – from you, perhaps – in order to avoid making rash decisions?

1 Ps 9:1, *The Message* **2** Cf Col 2:16–23; 1 Tim 4:1–5 **3** Cf Gen 9:4

WHAT KIND OF OBEDIENCE?

'May the words of my mouth and the meditation of my heart be pleasing in your sight, O Lord, my Rock and my Redeemer.'[1]

1 SAMUEL 15:1–16

To twenty-first century people like ourselves, the treatment of the Amalekites is horrific. How can God not just allow, but instruct Saul to bring about destruction on such a scale (v 3)? And for many today, the idea that this was a 'Holy War', with Saul carrying out God's sentence on them for their opposition to God's rescue of Israel from Egypt[2] only makes the matter worse. Yet before we rush to conclusions about God, we also have to face the fact that this same God against whom so many rail also gave his own Son to die for the world. It is often only when we see God's individual acts in the light of the whole that we really develop our faltering understanding of his character. And for some of us, our shouts against him may be muted when we face the contemporary destruction in which we are at least complicit by our silence. War is still all around us.

Amazingly, to contemporary Western minds at least, the text itself seems to be quite unconcerned with that issue. The big story is Saul's disobedience (v 9) and rejection by God, something which caused Samuel to spend the night agonising in prayer (v 11). For us, Saul's sin is easy to see. Sadly, it's so much easier to become angry and distressed over other people's sins and failings than over our own.

So Saul's similarity to us becomes apparent once again. He hadn't rejected the Lord or gone after another god. But like many of us he tried to serve God on his own terms. It was Saul's own decision to sacrifice the sheep and cattle which were already God's by right (v 15). And it was certainly Saul who chose to draw attention to himself (v 12) rather than God. Qualified obedience is so much easier than absolute obedience.

Ask God to show you any areas in your life where you are trying to have things both ways: being obedient but in your own way.

---

[1] Ps 19:14, NIV [2] Cf Exod 17:14–16; Num 24:20

RITUAL ESCAPISM

'If we confess our sins, he is faithful and just and will forgive us our sins and purify us from all unrighteousness.'[1]

1 SAMUEL 15:17–35

Saul's sin was worryingly simple. It wasn't so much what he did as what he didn't do (v 9). In fact, he could hardly see it as sin and claimed that he had obeyed God (v 20). But the detail he'd ignored was important – sins of omission can be as significant as sins of commission. His sin was a reflection of the reality of his heart, and Samuel told him that his rejection of God's word would be matched by God's rejection of him as king (v 23).

Samuel offered no comfort to Saul. Even though Saul recognised his sin, God's mind was made up (v 29) and the kingdom would in due course pass to another. In stark contrast to Saul, and in front of him to make the point, Samuel obediently undertook the awful task which Saul had avoided (vs 32,33). The act itself may have been out of character, but his obedience wasn't. Then, as Saul reached out to grab Samuel's cloak, he tore it, a powerful symbol of what would happen to his reign (vs 27,28).

The worrying thing about Saul is that on the surface, he hadn't rejected God at all. Worship had never seemed to be a problem for him and he seemed to do the right things (eg offering sacrifice, 13:9; fasting, 14:24; seeking guidance, 14:37). Unfortunately, ritual worship can be a replacement for an obedient life. Singing songs, praying prayers, feeling emotions, or in Saul's case offering sacrifices are all things that we can do relatively easily. But obedience? As far as God is concerned it is much more important than sacrifice (v 22). Disobedience is no less than idolatry, elevating the self to deity. No wonder Paul tells us to offer our bodies as a living sacrifice.[2] True worship encompasses the whole of our life, not just ritual, whether it be contemporary or traditional.

Think about your life today as a living sacrifice. Imagine offering it to God on an altar. How might that understanding change things?

[1] 1 John 1:9 [2] Rom 12:1

THE HEART OF THE MATTER

'Man looks at the outward appearance, but the LORD looks at the heart.'[1]

1 SAMUEL 16

Physical appearance is all-important in our visually mediated times – maybe we're not so different from the people of Samuel's era (v 7). But God has a different view on what really matters. Look out, in these verses, for the surprises God brings as he works out his agenda. First, watch Samuel's costly obedience. He had just experienced the trauma of dealing with the outcomes of Saul's disobedience[2] and is grieving for the effects it will have on his difficult protégé (v 1). Risking death as he goes to anoint Saul's successor – an act of treason – God provides him with an ironic get-out (vs 2,3; 15:22). Samuel, once in the place to which obedience has brought him, listens to God's voice, rather than the predictable ones of those around him (v 7).

Now look at how the Lord drives this story – both on a grand scale, and in the details of individuals' lives. The people had wanted a king. Now God intervenes with his choice (v 1). Unimportant Bethlehem, at the extreme end of Samuel's usual circuit, has special significance. Also home to Jesse's grandparents, Boaz and Ruth, it will later become known as the birthplace of their descendant, Jesus. God's unexpected choice of David is in keeping with what we know of God's character elsewhere in Scripture.[3] As David's calling is confirmed (v 13), so blessing departs from Saul (v 14). No longer God's anointed, Saul becomes an increasingly troubled and capricious despot. Whatever the exact meaning of 'an evil spirit from the LORD' (v 14), biblical scholars agree that the rejected 'chosen one' had become deeply depressed. Ironically, it is the presence and gifts of the one who will replace him that he brings into his life to soothe his pain (v 23). Obedience to God – or disobedience – will bring unexpected results as he works out his big plan and his purposes for our individual lives.

Whatever your outward appearance, what does God see in your heart? Pray for courage and faith to obey him as he leads you forward in his purposes.

[1] 1 Sam 16:7 (NIV) [2] 1 Sam 15 [3] eg 1 Cor 1:27–29

WHO'S THE CHAMPION?

'Surely God is my help; the Lord is the one who sustains me.'[1]

1 SAMUEL 17:1–27

Imagine the scene: two hills, two armies; the arrogant champion who, day after day, steps forward to challenge the Israelites with threats of servitude (v 9). In the face of such indomitable strength (v 4), Saul, the tall[2] but frightened king, can only feel terror (v 11). The Israelites had lost the plot. David the young brother, Joseph-like, has an apparently insignificant walk-on part (vs 17–19), but his understanding of the true nature of events is in sharp contrast with his fellow Israelites (v 26). It is this which triggers their deliverance and fresh momentum in the story of God's people. So, where do you find yourself in this scene? As we observe what the players in this story recognised about God, we can look for the implications for our own understanding of God, his activity in our own world and how we serve him today.

The Philistine champion was impressive: his appearance; his state-of-the-art, expensive combat equipment; his self-belief. But he did not understand who he was up against (vs 8–10). Mistakenly, he believed the terrified King Saul to be his likely opponent. But the joke was on him! Like the Israelites, we may sometimes be over-impressed by those who belittle our faith. Like them we too may forget who it is we serve. Enter the saviour from Bethlehem in Ephrathah (v 12). Young and inexperienced, David does not immediately impress, but he sees events with a clarity which eludes Saul's soldiers (v 24). The 'uncircumcised Philistine' indicates one who is relying on lifeless gods in contrast to the 'living God' of the Israelites (v 26). For the shepherd boy, the issue is clear: there is no match between the Philistines and God's army. David got things right with his single-minded confidence in God.

What battles are you facing? Ask God to give you a right understanding of who you are and the one whom you serve – then the courage to act.

---

1 Ps 54:4 **2** 1 Sam 10:23

IN GOD ALONE...

'It is not by sword or spear that the LORD saves; for the battle is the LORD's ...'[1]

1 SAMUEL 17:28–54

Age, position, experience, skills, appearance... all may bring respect and acclaim. But, as these verses teach, we should not be tempted to rely on any such human attributes. This is why David stands out – head and shoulders above the others spiritually. The words of Eliab, the oldest brother (v 28), reveal his heart and perhaps why he was not God's chosen one (16:6,7). His commonplace sibling jealousy blinds him to the rightness of his brother's passionate indignation and understanding of God. Saul, though impressed by David's words, at first can see only an inexperienced boy (v 33). Caught up in the conventions of the day, he insists on clothing David in armour. With reader hindsight, this may seem faintly ridiculous: God – or the too-big armour? Goliath knew what he was trusting in (17:5-7). The ill-equipped teenager was an infuriating insult (vs 42,44), but Goliath had not understood the true identity of his opponent – and he relied on things that are powerless by comparison.

Throughout, David affirms his trust in God alone (v 45). Drawing on past experience, he has grounds for trusting God (v 36). The stark contrast between the armour-clad champion and the young boy with his shepherd's sling makes it clear to everyone – Philistine and Israelite – that 'the battle is the LORD's' (vs 46,47). As the Philistine's god Dagon fell before God's ark,[2] so the Philistine falls before God's servant. Would they never learn! The accounts that follow raise some questions of chronology. However we explain them, we see here God's anointed one established for his future role as leader of God's people. David alone understood that they were on the Lord's side; he alone insisted on dependence on God – just a boy, but already a giant man of God.

What attributes do you admire – in yourself, or in others? Reflect on how far you, or your church, rely on these rather than trusting in God alone.

[1] 1 Sam 17:47 [2] 1 Sam 5:1–4

'A JEALOUS EYE'

Lord God, make me jealous for your glory, not my own.

1 SAMUEL 17:55 – 18:16

Jealousy is a terrible thing. Put aside for a moment the apparent inconsistencies in these ancient records and reflect instead on the causes of Saul's profound disturbance. David was the focus of this jealousy. Once, Saul had been the conquering hero.[1] Now, it's the newcomer who gets the popular vote. A wise leader would have been proud to have David at his side, but Saul cannot bear the tabloid headlines (vs 7-9). Aware of public feeling, he recognises the challenger for his throne - even though he apparently didn't know of David's earlier anointing.[2] There is an unbearable tension for Saul. At first he wants to keep this successful young man close to him - to bask in his glory? - but equally he is enraged by his success. No longer controlled by God's Spirit, evil takes over (vs 10,11). Biblical scholars aren't sure of the exact meaning here, but it's clear that without God, Saul's bitter jealousy grows into mad, murderous intent. He also has an increasing sense of isolation. Everyone loves David - Jonathan (v 1), David's fellow soldiers (v 5), all the people (v 16). Saul wrestles alone with his selfish fears (vs 12,15).

He could have responded differently. Jonathan, no mean soldier himself,[3] was willing to forgo his own status for David (v 4), despite the likely personal political cost, but Saul was unwilling to do the same. As well as David's self-evident achievements, did Saul's 'jealous eye' also recognise that 'the LORD was with David, but had departed from Saul' (v 12)? Today, safe in Christ, sin cannot ultimately destroy our relationship with God. Yet, if we choose to allow jealousy - or hatred or selfish concerns - to possess us, we also may feel a sense of loss of God's presence and peace as we wrestle with resulting destructive promptings towards others. Saul is a warning to us all.

Consider your feelings towards others – at work, in church, in your family. Confess any jealousy, asking the Holy Spirit to transform your thoughts so your words and actions reflect Christ's love.

[1] 1 Sam 11 [2] 1 Sam 16:1–13 [3] 1 Sam 14:1–23

BLESSED ARE THE PURE...

'Let the righteous rejoice in the LORD ... let all the upright in heart praise him!'[1]

1 SAMUEL 18:17–30

It had all looked so good for Saul – the self-effacing young warrior.[2] What had happened to turn him into this duplicitous, stay-at-home megalomaniac who thought only of maintaining his own position?

Jealousy had narrowed Saul's world. It wasn't God, the nation, their enemies or even his family which dominated Saul's life. Now what drove him was the desire to destroy the man he considered his enemy. Notice his deceitful scheming against the much-loved David (v 17 – not unlike David and Uriah a few years later[3]). Saul's publicly honey-coated words hid his dark motives. God's name, the Philistines and his daughters were used as mere devices to rid himself of the one he feared would take his throne (v 21). By contrast, David's demeanour towards the king is respectful and straightforward. He trusts Saul's motives, does not complain about broken promises, and is humble and brave. Unaware of the king's murderous plans, he calls his bluff by enthusiastically providing twice the bride-price (v 27)! Paradoxically, Saul's paranoid plans only served to confirm David in national prominence: more success, national renown (v 30) – and membership of the royal family. Again, we are given the clue to the diminished figure that Saul had become: he knew that the Lord was with David – and, by implication, not with him – and he was afraid (vs 28,29). No longer on the Lord's side, his enmity with David ruined his life.

The writer's skilful narrative reveals the falsity of the self-obsessed Saul. Yet, before rushing to condemn, let's consider whether we are ever guilty of using God's name or others' trust simply to advance our own cause. While David's later failings would drive him closer to God,[4] Saul would be increasingly captive to the self-protective fear which eventually led to his unhappy end.[5]

Confess any insincerity in your own life. Ask the Lord to make you a person 'after his own heart'.[6]

[1] Ps 64:10, NIV [2] 1 Sam 10:22,23; 11:13 [3] 2 Sam 11 [4] Pss 32,51 [5] 1 Sam 31 [6] 1 Sam 13:14

LOYALTY IN CONFLICT

Reflect on a time when a dispute between friends, colleagues or neighbours tested your loyalty to those involved.

Saul's desire to kill his son-in-law David is not shared by his son Jonathan, and daughter Michal. Out of deep affection for David, Jonathan persuades his father to revoke his death threat. Without alienating either party, Jonathan successfully mediates a reconciliation that enables David to return to Saul's court. Later, Michal foils her father's renewed attempt on David's life. On these occasions love wins out over hatred, as Jonathan and Michal courageously take a stand against the unjustified actions of their father, the king. When further conflict with the Philistines results in another victory for David, Saul's jealousy is rekindled and, in circumstances that mirror 1 Samuel 18:10,11, Saul once more attempts to spear David to death. Verse 9 provides a striking visual illustration of the differences between Saul and David. With a spear in his hand, Saul typifies the tyranny of aggression that promotes self-interest by annihilating others. With a harp in hand, David displays a servant attitude and brings healing to those in need. In my dealing with other people, whose interests come first? What's in my hand: a spear or a harp?

Set apart as the Lord's anointed, Saul was exceptionally privileged; this accounts for the uniqueness of certain incidents associated with him. However, the story of his life confirms Lord Acton's observation: 'Power tends to corrupt, and absolute power corrupts absolutely.' Although Saul, as king of Israel, has authority over others, even he remains subject to control by God, the divine king. While there is a complexity and mystery to God's dealings with Saul, as reflected in the differing effects of the Spirit of God upon him, the king's autonomy is not absolute. All this is a salient reminder that those who receive authority from God abuse it at their peril. Christian leaders beware!

'Blessed are the peacemakers.'[1] Is God calling you to mediate sensitively in a dispute at home, work or church?

[1] Matt 5:9; *cf* James 3:17,18

TRUE FRIENDS

Thank God for friends who can be relied upon for advice and support in the most trying of circumstances.

1 SAMUEL 20:1–23

Saul's death threat places David in an exceptionally difficult position. What is he to do next? Had I been in his shoes, how would I have responded? Remarkably, to discern the way forward he turns to Jonathan for help. In doing so David confidently anticipates that Jonathan will continue to place their friendship above loyalty to his father. Yet, this does not stop him from addressing those issues that are central to guaranteeing an enduring relationship.

David knows that his own personal integrity is vitally important in order to secure Jonathan's continued trust. For this reason he seeks Jonathan's reassurance that he has done Saul no harm. Jonathan must harbour no seeds of doubt about David's innocence, for such seeds could easily begin to grow in the context of a conflict between father and friend. For his part, Jonathan is concerned to assure David that he will be open and honest regarding his father's intentions. There will be no duplicity on Jonathan's part. He will communicate clearly and unambiguously how his father feels towards David. Through their frequent references to the Lord (vs 3,8,12,13,14,15,16,22,23) both men demonstrate that their desire for personal integrity and openness is integral to their religious convictions. Their loyalty to God affects deeply how they relate to one another and provides the secure foundation upon which their friendship rests.

This common commitment to God is clearly missing in Jonathan's relationship with his father, for Saul, as shown by his actions, has regrettably abandoned the Lord. Consequently, Jonathan's dealings with his father are less than transparent. Of necessity, he cannot be fully honest. On occasions, to protect the innocent from harm, we too may need to be discerning in how we act and guarded in what we say.

Heavenly Father, grant me discernment, faithfulness and wisdom that I may be a friend in whom others can have total confidence.

LIKE MOTHER, LIKE SON

Prayerfully ask God to speak to you in a meaningful way from this passage today.

David and Jonathan initiate their plan to ascertain Saul's present disposition towards David. Possibly they hope that Saul will relent and abide by the oath which he had earlier sworn to Jonathan.[1] When Saul eventually enquires about David's absence, his reaction reveals that he still longs to see him dead. His vitriolic outburst is clearly designed to win Jonathan over with a mixture of stick and carrot. Jonathan is a traitor – a trait obviously derived from his mother! If Jonathan was more like his father, and not a 'mummy's boy', he would stand up to the 'son of Jesse'. By deliberately avoiding David's name, Saul seeks to depersonalise him. He then attempts to entice Jonathan over to his side by highlighting how David is a threat to his son's future prospects as heir to the throne. If David lives, Jonathan will never be king. Although Saul maligns Jonathan's behaviour as 'perverse and rebellious', his own actions are hardly exemplary.

In spite of Saul's tirade, Jonathan holds his nerve. When the king speaks of David's death, Jonathan raises two important questions: 'Why should he be put to death? What has he done?' But there is no reasoning with Saul on this occasion.[2] He answers Jonathan with a spear. Ironically, Jonathan's life is now endangered, not by David, but by his own father. His support for David brings him into conflict with his father and almost results in his death. Centuries later, David's 'Greater Son' reveals that loyalty to him would sometimes result in rejection by one's own family.[3] To follow Jesus requires courageous determination. The contrast between Jonathan's public encounter with his father and his secret meeting with David could not be greater. David's obeisance, kisses and tears reveal a genuine love and respect for his friend. Once more their shared experience of God binds them together.

In some cultures the cost of following Jesus is alienation from one's family. Pray for those who must make this difficult choice.

[1] 1 Sam 19:6 [2] Contrast 1 Sam 19:4–6 [3] Matt 10:34–39

NO HIDING PLACE

'Your word is a lamp to my feet and a light for my path.'[1] Praise God for how he directs our lives.

1 SAMUEL 21

Wanted by Saul, David soon discovers that it is not easy to find a secure place of refuge. His flight takes him from one extreme to the other. By going to Nob, David seeks refuge at the Lord's sanctuary. However, Ahimelek's anxious reaction suggests that he is aware of Saul's decision to kill David. No doubt David quickly sensed that he could not rely on the priest for protection. Ahimelek's fear of Saul may explain why David craftily claims that he is on royal business, the details of which must remain secret.

From the Lord's sanctuary in Nob David goes to the Philistine city of Gath. Having previously killed the Philistine champion Goliath, David's journey to enemy territory further underlines the danger he faced in his own land. By deserting Saul and taking back Goliath's sword[2] David possibly hopes to gain acceptance. However, when Achish's servant describes David as 'the king of the land' (v 11), he realises that Achish will view him as a dangerous threat. His best protection is to act insane. Ironically, far from being out of his mind, David's cunning saves his life.

Before both the Israelite priest and the Philistine king, David is less than fully honest. In different ways he deceives both men. How should we judge his actions? It is exceptionally easy to condemn his deception from the comfort and security of an armchair. But desperate situations sometimes require desperate measures. We would baulk at condemning as a thief the concentration camp prisoner who pilfers food to feed a starving inmate. And Jesus certainly wasn't embarrassed by David's actions. On the contrary he uses this passage to counter the Pharisees' unjustified condemnation of his own disciples.[3]

Consider how Matthew 12:7 might temper your judgement of others when you perceive them as doing wrong.

---

[1] Ps 119:105 [2] Though not explicitly stated, this seems to be implied [3] See Matt 12:1–4

CONSPIRACY THEORIES

Lord of light and truth, shine into my darkness and dispel all falsehood.

I recall visiting a student flat that had an intriguing poster near its front door. It reassuringly read: 'Just because you're paranoid doesn't mean they're not out to get you.' What would Saul have made of this? Blinded by jealousy of David, he imagines conspiracies where none exist.

When David relocates to the forest of Hereth, Saul's frustration at not being able to capture the 'son of Jesse' (v 8) causes him to berate his main supporters, his fellow tribesmen. To bolster his authority, Saul had bought their support through gifts of fields and vineyards, some of which may have belonged previously to the 400 men who now follow David. Obviously, David is not the only victim of Saul's regime. Typical of tyrants everywhere, Saul detects conspiracies where there are none. Doeg's intervention is astute. By pointing the finger at Ahimelek he confirms – for tyrants are always right – Saul's worst suspicion, but clears those presently being charged. Although Doeg is truthful, the truth is manipulated to evil ends in order to gain the king's favour. Later, when Saul's officials are rightly reluctant to kill the priests, Doeg has no such qualms. Blind obedience to a tyrant often results in the death of the innocent. Our world has witnessed too many Doegs.

Ultimately, however, Saul is the one who must carry the blame for the slaughter of Ahimelek and the inhabitants of Nob. His paranoia deafens him to Ahimelek's plea of innocence and colours his judgement. Even if the priest had in some way conspired with David, the punishment meted out is excessive in the extreme. The actions of Saul and Doeg stand in sharp contrast to David's willingness to take responsibility for the slaughter of Ahimelek's family. When it comes to taking a stand, am I a Doeg or a David?

Reflect on Doeg's use of the truth. Confess to God those times when you have used the truth to injure others.

GUIDED BY GOD

Thank God for the leadership provided by people you know who walk closely in step with God.

1 SAMUEL 23:1–14

The author of Samuel frequently contrasts the actions of Saul and David. The account of Saul's destruction of Nob is immediately followed by a description of David's deliverance of Keilah, a city located close to the Philistine border south-east of Gath. Not surprisingly, the men supporting David have little desire to bring upon themselves the wrath of the Philistines; they are already fugitives from Saul. Confronting two enemies will not be easy. In the light of this, David exercises tremendous faith in God. In going to rescue the inhabitants of Keilah, he exhibits unselfish compassion and courageous leadership, qualities that set him apart from Saul.

David also differs from Saul in his desire to be guided by God, an important motif in this passage. While we are not told in detail how David ascertained God's will, he received clear guidance. On several occasions, he looks to confirm God's support for an action that he is already contemplating. This is especially so in the second half of the passage when David's questions require a 'Yes' or 'No' answer. God's response may well have been given using lots, like the Urim and Thummim, which were associated with the high priest's clothing. This could explain why David calls for the ephod (v 9). Unlike David, Saul does not enquire of the Lord. While he arrogantly presumes that God will hand David over to him (v 7) the exact opposite happens (v 14). It is all too easy to presuppose wrongly that my will is God's will.

While David endangers his own life in order to save the inhabitants of Keilah, they are presented as very fickle. Probably aware of what Saul has done to the town of Nob, they are prepared to betray David in order to save their own lives. True loyalty is often rare, and we need to beware of trusting others too easily.[1]

Pray for those in positions of leadership that they will be constantly and consistently seeking God's guidance.

---

[1] Matt 10:16

CLOSER THAN A BROTHER

Recall a time when someone displayed sacrificial love to you in a time of personal difficulty. Thank God for such friendship.

1 SAMUEL 23:15–29

In spite of his faith in God, the constant pressure of being a fugitive begins to sap David's inner strength. He lives each day with the knowledge that Saul has harnessed all his royal resources with the sole purpose of annihilating him. Saul's attack on the citizens of Nob possibly added to David's anxiety, for he realises that his presence may result in innocent people being put to death. In the light of these factors, the strain on David is enormous. He is close to breaking point. Remarkably, it is Jonathan, Saul's son, who daringly seeks David out in order to encourage him. From start to finish, Jonathan's actions are God-centred: he helps David to find strength in God and together they make a covenant before the Lord. In all this Jonathan graciously places David and his needs ahead of his own. Jonathan is a true pastor to David. Here is Christ-like love in action.[1]

The depth of Jonathan's commitment to David is contrasted with the Ziphites' willingness to hand David over to Saul. Located to the south-east of Keilah, in the hill country of Judah, Ziph was inhabited by fellow tribesmen of David. Given Jonathan's support for David, their lack of family solidarity is especially striking. While Jonathan comes to David, they go to Saul, offering to hand David over to him. Even among his own kinsmen David cannot rest in safety. Friendships in God can often be closer than family loyalties.

Aided by the Ziphites, Saul's pursuit of David comes close to success. However, as the king's troops close in on their prey, an invasion by the Philistines proves timely. Although the narrator does not say so explicitly, David's rescue from Saul is providential. No doubt there are many times when our heavenly Father has rescued us from disaster. Often we may not even have realised it. Give thanks with a grateful heart.

Reflect on Jonathan's pastoral care of David. Is there someone to whom you can be a Jonathan today?

[1] 1 John 3:16

LOVE YOUR ENEMY

'While we were God's enemies, we were reconciled to him through the death of his Son ...'[1] Praise God for his reconciling love.

1 SAMUEL 24

Saul's pursuit of David continues unabated. With an elite force that outnumbers David's followers five to one, Saul pursues David to En Gedi on the western side of the Dead Sea. In this inhospitable region of cliffs and ravines, David and his men take refuge in one of the many caves there. When Saul seeks privacy in the same cave to relieve himself, David's followers see this as a God-given opportunity to take the king's life. Was God, as he had promised, not handing Saul over to David? How easy for David to slay his enemy!

Higher moral values, however, influence David's actions. Even so, he realises that his behaviour is not perfect. His conscience troubles him for having cut the corner of the king's robe. The disclosure of his presence to Saul requires incredible courage. It would surely have been much safer to remain in hiding. Yet, risking his own life, David bravely outlines why he is innocent and undeserving of death. The evidence is so compelling that even Saul is forced to acknowledge David's superior righteousness and his own malevolence. Remarkably, Saul discerns that his opponent's moral virtues will inevitably establish him as king (v 20). By risking everything, David wins the day, and the manner of this victory is noteworthy. In business or office life, God may sometimes call us to similar boldness.[2]

David respects Saul's God-given status as king and does nothing to undermine his royal authority. On the contrary, his actions and words emphasise his commitment to be a loyal subject. Highlighting the importance of Saul's status as the Lord's anointed, David describes himself as a dead dog, a flea (v 14). Not only is David's present humility and future kingship reminiscent of his 'greater Son',[3] but his behaviour is a challenging example for us to follow.

Heavenly Father, when others put me under pressure to act inappropriately, give me the moral courage to do what is right in your eyes.

[1] Rom 5:10 [2] Prov 28:1 [3] Phil 2:5–11; *see also* J Montgomery, 1771–1854, 'Hail to the Lord's Anointed'

A SHORT FUSE!

Praise God that he is 'a gracious and compassionate God, slow to anger and abounding in love'.[1]

The final seven chapters of this book are framed by the deaths of Samuel and Saul, both significant events in the story of God's people. Samuel has recently died and his loss is deeply mourned by the Israelites. We don't know how this impacted David but we have a possible clue when we see him acting out of character in reaction to Nabal's obstructive behaviour and rudeness. Admittedly, hospitality for 600 men would have been a costly business[2] but sheep shearing was usually a time of celebration[3] and Nabal, a very wealthy man, certainly owed David a favour.

Up until now David has been a model of patience in his dealings with Saul, refusing to retaliate or fight back, but with Nabal it's a very different matter. He goes into overdrive with an energy fuelled by deep anger. Taking 400 armed men with him he sets out to teach Nabal a lesson. His 'self-restraint had gone to pieces and a few insulting words have made him see red!'[4]

Conflict is a fact of life. People say and do things that make us cross, yet sadly there is little teaching in our churches about how to deal with this very raw human emotion. We often equate being a Christian with 'niceness'. This can lead us to deny the anger we feel, burying it within, only for it to re-emerge at a different time or fester inside, turning into bitterness.[5] The Bible has a lot to say about anger. Anger is recognised as something not to deny, but rather to handle rightly. We are to be like our God in being slow to anger and avoiding reacting negatively under stress, irrespective of how justified our anger might feel. And we are to make every effort to resolve the matter[6] rather than covering up our feelings with a veneer of Christian respectability.

With a Bible concordance, do a word study on 'anger', asking God to show you how you need to change and grow in handling anger rightly.

---

[1] Jonah 4:2 [2] DF Payne, *NBCR*, IVP, 1970, p300 [3] 1 Sam 25:8; 2 Sam 13:23,24
[4] C Swindoll, *David*, Word, 1997 [5] Eph 4:31; Heb 12:15 [6] Eph 4:26

BEING PEACEMAKERS

Ask Jesus to fill you with his peace afresh as something for you to possess and give away to others today.

1 SAMUEL 25:23–44

This is the stuff of TV soap operas. We have the bad guy, Nabal, a belligerent and self-centred individual with a reputation for meanness. His name means 'fool' referring to a person who says 'there is no God'.[1] We have Abigail, his beautiful, intelligent and gracious wife, whom he clearly doesn't deserve. Lastly there is the hero, David, the honourable yet wronged leader with his band of men. The story itself is about effective mediation and its impact and also 'relates how David became a property owner in Judah, telling us too of the beginnings of the royal harem. Theologically, verses 28–31 are the most significant.'[2] In these verses Abigail pleads with David not to do anything rash that might endanger or even destroy the lasting dynasty that God will give him. Looking into the future, Abigail alludes (v 30) to the Davidic covenant,[3] to the time when the Lord will have done for David 'every good thing he promised concerning him'. God has already appointed him leader, a fact earlier announced to Saul by Samuel,[4] but David would not exercise effective rule over Israel until after Saul's death.

Abigail put herself at risk, placing herself between her husband and David. She did this thoughtfully and intentionally, carefully preparing what she thought could turn the situation around. Her approach was one of generosity and humility, acknowledging the wrong that had been done but appealing to David to consider the implications of his response in light of the bigger picture of God's long-term intentions.

Mediating between people can be difficult, costly and time-consuming, but our calling as Christians is to be 'peacemakers'[5] in the way Abigail was – when family members no longer talk to each other, churches are divided by conflict, and neighbours fall out. Our choice is to be either part of the problem or part of the solution…

Pray for people to be raised up to mediate in current international war zones, asking God to help you become an effective 'peacemaker' too.

[1] Ps 53:1 [2] Payne, *NBCR*, p300 [3] 2 Sam 7 [4] 1 Sam 13:14 [5] Matt 5:9; James 3:17,18

THE BIGGER PICTURE

'The real voyage of discovery consists not in seeking new landscapes but in having new eyes.'[1] Pray for eyes of faith today.

1 SAMUEL 26

Saul is obsessed with David and unable to throw off his paranoia about him. Again he pursues David to kill him, yet as on previous occasions in this encounter we find Saul deeply ambivalent in his feelings. It is David's grace, his refusal to retaliate although having full opportunity, which confounds Saul's distorted reasoning about David as a personal threat.

Repeatedly David had been pushed to his limits by Saul and must have felt great personal hurt from the overt hostility and rejection of this man he had previously looked up to and seen as something of a 'father figure'. On top of this, his fugitive status had resulted in him being exiled from the land of Israel, and so excluded from sharing in the communal life of God's people and their worship of him (v 19). Despite all this, David's attitudes and reactions were radically shaped by his high view of Saul's position as king, seeing his importance in the context of the bigger picture of God's anointing of him. Whilst priests were also anointed, it is usually the king who is referred to as 'the anointed of the LORD'.[2] Anointing signified separation to the Lord for a particular task and divine equipping for that task. When Saul was anointed by Samuel, he was designated by the Lord to be the nation's leader and chief in rank.[3]

Tragically, Saul in his latter years lost sight of the bigger picture of God's purposes for his life, becoming instead inward-looking and defensive. Saul is not alone in this. Leadership roles in church or the workplace can become an end in themselves, positions to be maintained in the face of pressure. The reasons may be understandable, but when we lose sight of the bigger picture of God's hand on our life, with good purposes for us,[4] then we're in trouble just as Saul was!

Prayerfully decide that you are going to be someone who encourages others to keep in view the 'big picture', asking for sensitivity to do so...

[1] Marcel Proust, novelist and critic, 1871–1922 [2] Exod 29:7; 40:12–15; 1 Sam 24:6; Ps 2:2–6 [3] 1 Sam 10:1 [4] Rom 8:28

2 SAMUEL

2 Samuel has sometimes been regarded as the court chronicles of David. We are told about his successes, his failures and sins, and in particular, the treachery and domestic strife he had to endure. Yet embedded in this story is a promise which found its fulfilment in Christ. David was not just God's choice for that time; he was to head up a line which would lead to the Messiah himself.[1] David was a leader whose men would protect and follow him to the death.[2] He dealt fairly with others and showed kindness and generosity (eg his dealings with Mephibosheth[3]). His behaviour demonstrates something of God's gracious dealings with us.

David believed God and trusted him. We find him regularly praying and seeking God's guidance, praising him and expressing his gratitude. David's psalms illustrate the depth of his relationship with God.[4] He wasn't perfect though. He gave in to sin and temptation. Yet, when he was in the wrong, he was quick to repent and put things right with God.[5] In his faithfulness, his courage, his trust in God, his human weakness and repentance, David provides us with many encouraging and challenging examples as to how we too should walk with our God.

Outline

1 Sad news about Saul	1:1–27
2 David over Judah	2:1 – 4:12
3 The kingdom consolidated	5:1 – 9:13
4 Victory and defeat	10:1 – 12:31
5 Civil war	13:1 – 20:26
6 About Gibeonites and Philistines	21:1–22
7 David's testimony	22:1 – 23:7
8 David's mighty men	23:8–39
9 David counts his people	24:1–25

[1] Luke 2:11 [2] 2 Sam 23:8 [3] 2 Sam 9:1–13 [4] Ps 23 [5] 2 Sam 12:13; Ps 32

DEATH WITHOUT GLORY

'Risen, ascended, glorified'[1] – reflect on life after death as Jesus shows the way to the Father.

2 SAMUEL 1:1–16

The account of Saul's death as recounted by the Amalekite is at odds with that in 1 Samuel 31, but the writer puts them side by side and leaves the reader to judge. There is careful use of irony, alerting us to read between the lines. Why was an Amalekite, an enemy of Israel, assisting in Saul's request to hasten his death (vs 9,10)? Is his account believable, and does David take it at face value?

No wonder David expresses genuine grief. Even though Saul had been his enemy, David mourns his loss. A leader, handsome, brave, chosen by God through prophetic appointment, anointed (*mashiach* = Messiah), he had all the promise and possibility of a great leader – but he died depressed, deserted and suicidal. The killing of the messenger is the opposite of the reward he hoped for, but expresses David's deep emotions and his judgement of the Amalekite's motives and character. David himself will have to watch his motives and actions, and if this is an overreaction it speaks of the difficulties David will create for himself later in his reign. We must be careful, when hearing bad news, to distinguish between the facts as they are reported, the emotional response we express, and the correct course of action, avoiding thoughtless responses.

We are left in no doubt of the key fact, the death of Saul, a life which promised much but delivered little. In Jewish life, mourning, even over enemies, is a serious responsibility. It is marked by the tearing of garments (v 2). There is a week of complete break from ordinary life and work, followed by a month of intermediate mourning and a full year of sadness after the death of a loved one. Saul's departure must be appropriately marked, before David can get on with the task God has called him to.

How do you express the deepest emotions of grief and loss? How can we comfort others?

1 From George H Bourne, 1874, 'Lord, enthroned in heavenly splendour'

GODLY GRIEF

'Blessed are those who mourn, for they will be comforted.'[1] Lift yourself and others to God in prayer.

2 SAMUEL 1:17–27

In recent years, many areas of Britain have been devastated by unprecedented floods, the result of climate change and global warming. Politicians blame one another for failing to prepare for the disaster, and the media present stories of panic buying – and stories of personal courage. The Jewish response to such disasters is also to lament. David sets himself, and his whole tribe, to lament the deaths of Saul and Jonathan. Giving expression to grief is not just a healthy and wholesome psychological reaction to bereavement, but there are also political and spiritual aspects to the poem of verses 19–27. It encapsulates the grief of a nation at the loss of their king, and pays appropriate tribute to the departed, refusing to speak ill of them. In ancient times the king symbolised the life of the nation, and while Saul viewed David as his enemy, David astutely refuses to criticise his former persecutor. He must follow in his footsteps, and he wants the crown to be held in respect.

The book of Jashar[2] must have held many such national songs, of both mourning and thanksgiving. One third of the psalms follow the lament pattern, often a circular meditation that begins and ends with expressions of grief, and includes calling on God, statements of confidence in previous acts of rescue and mercy, and even calling for judgement on enemies. David's lament here includes no note of judgement or recrimination. He will not speak ill of the dead, and genuinely mourns Saul and his covenant-partner Jonathan as the better of them deserved. How do we lament? Do we express grief wholesomely, prayerfully, and with God's larger vision of our situation in mind?

Write a lament, either over the loss of a loved one, or a situation of national or spiritual tragedy. Use the lament as a form of prayer, or turn it into a song.

[1] Matt 5:4 [2] Josh 10:12,13

THE PATH TO POWER

'Thine be the glory, risen, conquering Son!'[1] Reflect on the power of the cross.

2 SAMUEL 2:1–17

Grieving over, David sets his sights on the throne promised to him by Samuel.[2] It is no easy progression from outlaw and mercenary to ruling in Jerusalem over the 12 tribes. David must plan his moves carefully. No wonder he begins with prayer (v 1). There follows a combination of intrigue, violence and cunning, combined with the working out of God's purposes for king, people and land. Our assessment of the moral aspects of David's actions should be carefully weighed, and his motives seen for what they are, not whitewashed or over-spiritualised. How do we evaluate the lives of contemporary Christian and political leaders, and what does this teach us about our own lives? The Lord's guidance comes through taking hold of circumstances. Hebron, a fortified location in the south, has benefited from being the base for David's raiding parties, and is ready to welcome him as he set up a local reign over the southern tribes for seven years, before locating to Jerusalem. His public coronation (v 4) is in contrast to the secret ceremony performed by Samuel, and calls for recognition and support.

The northern tribes will be the real problem. Loyalty to Saul's line continues, and as David is crowned king in the south, Abner makes Ish-Bosheth (v 8; *bosheth* means 'shame'[3]) king, continuing the civil war between Saul's supporters and David's.

Previously rescued by Saul,[4] the men of Jabesh Gilead now rescue his body and bury him with due honour.[5] David, rather than impose his authority over them, seeks to persuade them to join his side. The same loving kindness they showed Saul, David asks the Lord to show to them, and he promises to treat them with faithfulness. Their previous loyalty to Saul is transferred, but will not last.

'In their hearts human beings plan their course, but the Lord establishes their steps.'[6] How do your motives match your actions?

[1] Edmond Budry, 1854–1932   [2] 1 Sam 16:1–13   [3] A euphemism for 'Baal'
[4] 1 Sam 11:1–11   [5] But *see* 2 Sam 21:12   [6] Prov 16:9

WARS AND WIVES

'When I survey the wondrous cross.'[1] How may I give myself, in response to what God has given me in Jesus?

2 SAMUEL 2:18 – 3:5

David's character is shown in this section by the behaviour of his men, and the increase of his family. As the power of Saul's followers declines, David's grows, but there is little to distinguish the methods, motives or message that they send. The divine plans for David's eventual rule are worked out in scenes of battle and bedroom that are not to be commended, but should be viewed critically. The human flaws we see in powerful men are apparent. The war as the continuation of politics by violent means gives us insight into the struggle for power.

Scenes of violence flash daily across our TV screens. Conflict is an everyday reality in many parts of the world, but the horror, brutality and loss of life that war brings cannot be excused. So when the 'play' of the previous verses (2:14) becomes loss of life, the tragedy of tribe against tribe intensifies. The grim details of Abner's reluctance to fight a younger, less experienced warrior, and the unnecessary killing speak volumes. Abner knew that killing him would result in Joab's need for revenge. The conflict between families loyal to either David or Saul spelt doom for the prospect of peace or a united kingdom.

Strife between tribes is offset with David's taking of wives and the birth of sons. Despite the warnings of Deuteronomy 17, David consolidates his power base by accumulating wives. This is not just the sign of an unrestrained sexual appetite but also evidence of shrewd political calculation. A wife in every tribe gives an insurance policy against betrayal and an assurance of loyalty from the families involved, but the number of wives eager for their children's advancement will eventually be the ruin of David and his line in battles for succession after his death. Civil war will again result from David's inability to control his household, just as his failure to prevent the fighting between Abner and Joab speaks volumes.

How can we control our appetites for money, sex and power?

1 Isaac Watts, 1674–1748

REVENGE AND GRIEF

'Forgive us our sins, for we also forgive everyone who sins against us.'[1]

'The enemy of my enemy is my friend' – so it is said – but here the complexities of the power struggle set Joab and David at odds, as Abner's change of sides from Saul to David results in his death at the hands of Joab. As Saul's cousin and commander of his army,[2] Abner is uniquely placed to influence the outcome of the conflict. He can deliver Saul's army, has power to make Ish-Bosheth king after Saul's death, and can claim the throne for himself by acquiring Saul's concubine, Rizpah. Rebuked by Ish-Bosheth, Abner defects to David.

Abner's visit to David to arrange David's accession to the throne results in his own death, as Joab takes revenge for the death of his brother Asahel, or in reaction to the threat posed to his own leadership of the army should David favour the new recruit. The passage states that David deliberately mourns Abner, demonstrating that he had no part in his murder, but the murky waters of political intrigue around David do not allow him to emerge guiltless either. He has not the power to restrain Joab's thirst for revenge – or perhaps he allows it.

People like Abner and Joab are examples to us of the fight for power and influence that we see throughout society and church life. We use words of malicious gossip to destroy the characters of those we disagree with – and possibly their careers as well. Conflict in life is inevitable, and often costly. How can we make peace with those we are opposed to? In Israel today, as in many parts of the world, the quest for peace, reconciliation and justice in the face of ongoing conflict is much needed. Only with God's help can it succeed.

Who do I need to be at peace with today? How can my personal conflicts be resolved?

---

[1] *Cf* Matt 6:12; Luke 11:4 [2] 1 Sam 14:50

HARD CHOICES

How do you handle difficult relationships?

2 SAMUEL 4

With Abner's death, Ish-Bosheth, the man he had anointed as king (2:8–10), had no protection. Now the two-year reign of the rival king comes to an abrupt end. His own men murder him while he is in bed. We are not spared the gruesome, macabre details of his betrayal, stabbing and decapitation, as the narrator wants us to experience the outrage that David will express over the assassination (v 11).

Saul's line posed a potential threat to any claim David had to the throne, despite his anointing by Samuel and acceptance by the southern tribes. David wants to act magnanimously to Saul's house out of friendship for Jonathan and recognition of God's earlier choice of Saul, but his supporters are mired in the real politic of gangland-type killings in their desire to put their leader in power. This is not the kingship David wants or God commands. David has them put to death.

There are no bloodless revolutions in the Bible, and we should recognise that although God allows such raw political and military activity he does not condone it. David's hands are stained with blood, despite his protest here. He has survived by God's help, but also used his wits to form some shady alliances, outmanoeuvre his opponents, and accumulate wives. When he comes to the throne, he will have to face up to the consequences of his actions.

Personally, we recognise the hard choices life brings to us on many issues. Here David's transition from rebel leader to military statesman to peacemaker and king is set before us for our benefit.[1] His character is refined by the experience of leadership, and he must set an example that will allow his own reign to proceed without assassination attempts and instability. Power must be exercised wisely, with a longing to please God, who knows the heart.

What difficult decisions do you face today? How does God see your motivations?

[1] Rom 15:4

CITY OF OUR GOD

Read or sing one of the psalms about Jerusalem (Psalms 46, 47 or 48). What does it say to you?

The long march to power is over. The shepherd boy of Bethlehem is now 'shepherd' (v 2) of his people (a common term in the ancient world for the monarch). The ten northern tribes acknowledge his authority, previously accepted only by Judah and Benjamin. David has been with them in weakness ('flesh') and in strength ('bone', v 1, NRSV), and they love him and are ready to serve him.

David's first move is the capture of Jerusalem and its selection as capital. This was a brilliant decision. Jerusalem is strategically important and militarily defensible. It does not come under any one tribe, as the Jebusites still possess it. Once captured, it will belong to all, and unite them all. It is ideal as a base for David, combining fortress and palace. It will become a worship centre and place of pilgrimage. The tradition of Abraham's offering of Isaac on Mount Moriah, and the image popular in the ancient world of the divine presence enthroned on mountain-top cities, will all build the mystique of Jerusalem, not just as capital for David and his offspring but as a future place of pilgrimage for all nations.

As I write, a new round of talks between Israel and the Palestinians begins. Can such a fought-over city as Jerusalem become the focus of peace, justice, reconciliation and security? Or will it remain a cause of dispute and bloodshed? We are to pray for the peace of Jerusalem,[1] and to pursue peace.[2] Whatever our understandings of future prophetic fulfilment of God's purposes for Israel and the nations, we must acknowledge the vital significance that Jerusalem still plays politically. Pray that great David's greater Son may establish his kingdom 'on earth as it is in heaven', beginning with Jerusalem and extending to all the nations.

Which areas of my life need physical and spiritual defence? Where is the place of unity in my life? Who is in command? Who has the victory?

[1] Ps 122:6 [2] 1 Pet 3:11; Ps 34:14

DEATH AND DANCING

'For the LORD has chosen Zion, he has desired it for his dwelling ...'[1]
Worship in awe at our God's longing to live among his people.

2 SAMUEL 6

The Ark of the Covenant was the holiest object in Israel's life and worship, containing the two tablets of the Ten Commandments, Aaron's budding rod and a golden urn filled with manna.[2] The word *aron* means 'cupboard' or 'throne', and as no image could be made of God, his throne was awesome in the way it suggested his presence. The Song of the Ark[3] showed its importance, not just in worship in the Tabernacle, but in battle. David wishes to consolidate military and spiritual authority in his newly formed capital, so it must be brought to Jerusalem.

Abinadab lived in Kiriath Jearim, where the Ark rested for 20 years, after it was recaptured from the Philistines.[4] David's plans are threatened by the rash behaviour of Uzzah, and a further delay takes place. The holiness of the Ark must not be taken lightly. Psalm 132 expresses David's longings, his feelings and his worship as he reflected on what it meant to bring the Ark to Jerusalem.

I have sat many times at night on the hilltop of Kiriath Jearim, looking out on the lights of Jerusalem some nine miles away. Today Abu Ghosh is an Arab village (with great restaurants!) that lives in peace with her Israeli neighbours, and a church is built on the hill where the Ark rested. My prayers echo the longing David had, to see the presence of God return to Jerusalem. Not an empty throne, but a risen King to be greeted with dancing and enthusiastic worship. David, for all his faults, had his heart in the right place. We cannot be negative, like Michal (v 20), when God is on the move. We may not let our hair down, like David, but our desire for God's presence, power and peace in our lives should be the longing of our hearts.

Make a study of the Ark in Scripture – how does its significance compare with the incarnation of Jesus? How do you celebrate God's presence?

---

[1] Ps 132:13 [2] Heb 9:4; Num 17:1–11; Exod 16:33,34 [3] Num 10:35,36
[4] 1 Sam 5:1,2

DON'T RUN AHEAD OF GOD

Do not rush into your time with God to 'get it done', but take time; be still in his presence, perhaps play some quiet music.

2 SAMUEL 7:1–17

After 20 turbulent years, David surveys a united kingdom, a secure capital, with God's Ark at its centre. All his dreams have been fulfilled. When you have lived on adrenalin, though, it is easier to create new projects to fill the vacuum than to stop when the obvious challenges are past.

Here David compares the tent in which the Ark resides unfavourably with his palace (as Haggai does later[1]). What drives David to want to do something – embarrassment, pity or a desire to do something for God, who has helped him so much? Whatever his motive, his desire to give to God is genuine, and received as such by God's spokesman, Nathan. Welcoming the generosity of spirit, Nathan endorses the proposal. However, that night, Nathan receives a rude awakening and discovers that not all good plans are God's plans. The tent was God's idea, not an economy measure by a previous generation. It allowed for mobility and symbolised the identification of God with his people in all their struggles. God had not asked for anything more. More importantly, the people needed to understand that the rise of shepherd boy to king was God's doing, not David's. God had been in charge throughout.

The Lord reigns and David is his servant. Furthermore, God is not finished with him yet. A building project at this stage would divert attention from God's intended work of building a 'house' for David, securing David's line and future. God would exchange a tent for a temple – but not now, and not through David. This vision for the future would see partial fulfilment in his son Solomon, and ultimate fulfilment in his greater Son, Jesus, and the inauguration of the kingdom of God. Sometimes we need to listen to God before we pursue our own agendas!

What plans are you making? Do you look for God's endorsement of your plans or do you expect him to lead you into his will?

[1] Hag 2:2,3

'NO' IS AN ANSWER

Reflect on God's purposes, from creation to consummation. Let that move you to worship. Praise him before you read today.

2 SAMUEL 7:18–29

Knock-backs are always hard to take, at any time in life. They are especially hard when you have become accustomed to people taking your ideas as instructions. How you handle such reversals is very revealing of your character. King David has just been put firmly in his place, his plans discarded. Credit is due to Nathan for not holding anything back. He had got it wrong, and acted immediately to curb David's enthusiasm. But how would David respond?

Here we see the quality of David, for he did not pout but went straight into God's presence and sat down. It is impossible to get some people to simply stop and reflect. Such an exercise can be profitable – especially so when you go into God's presence and reflect on what God has said. There, free of the constant demands on him as king, David took time to pray and, in that prayer, owned God's word to him through Nathan. He had got things out of perspective, and he now saw his grandiose scheme as the limited thing it was. Leaders are often tempted into building projects to leave some permanent record of their time. They can be a distraction from the more important work God wants to do in people's lives.

Through Nathan's words, David is brought into a different dimension. Almost breathlessly, he sees God's plan for his people down through the ages and his own life within that framework. For most of us, our significance can only be found against a broader canvas than our own lifetime. Seeing God at work, in history and experience, David shelves his plans without hesitation and embraces God's purpose. Perhaps he recognises that whereas the temple project would have brought him honour, the newly revealed plans ensure that the glory is correctly directed, to God himself.

'Have Thine own way, Lord ... / Thou art the Potter, I am the clay. / Mould me and make me, after Thy will / While I am waiting, yielded and still.'[1]

[1] Adelaide A Pollard, 1862–1934

YOUR KINGDOM COME

Pray through the Lord's Prayer carefully, considering each petition as you pray it, seeing how it will affect your life today.

This is a difficult chapter for us, one that we instinctively react against. It is one thing to pray, 'Your kingdom come,' another to realise its full implications. For generations, warfare between the tribes and nations around Israel had brought misery and insecurity. As always in war zones, the vulnerable suffered the most, their homes destroyed, their fields pillaged, their lives threatened. The time had come to end such skirmishes and deal with regional anarchy.

David is not a ceremonial king but a determined ruler. He fights to win, to enforce that peace through which prosperity may come. But he cannot do this without the use of force. Chapter 8 spells out in graphic detail what war involves, even when the Lord is giving the victory. It is a violent, bloodthirsty business. There is a toughness in this chapter; the recurring bouts of ruthless engagement, separated by years of fragile peace and temporary truces, have to come to an end. At last a king has emerged who will take charge of both south and north. Defeat of David's enemies is followed by imposed rule. The wealth, gold, silver and bronze taken in plunder and tribute is dedicated to God, to be used in the future building of the Temple.

Key to this chapter is the kind of rule that follows. David did 'what was just and right for all his people' (v 15). He was from Judah, but he cared for the welfare of all the people, not just some. For good to flourish, a blind eye cannot be turned to evil. Having conquered, the challenge for David was whether he could handle the responsibility of power. The answer here is that he could and he did. I wonder whether that could always be said of us.

Peacemaking is costly, but there may relationships we need to sort out before they eat away at every other aspect of our lives. Do it now.

CHECK YOUR GUEST LIST

Count your blessings, so that you can remind yourself of all that God has done for you and continues to do each day. Then worship him.

2 SAMUEL 9

In this remarkable story, an incident from the past casts a long shadow. David had made a promise to his best friend, Jonathan; now it had to be kept. He did not try to water it down or wriggle out of its implications. Power would twist in his hands unless he used it not only to impose force, but also to demonstrate thoughtfulness and practical kindness. So he took the initiative and uncovered the sad story of Mephibosheth, Jonathan's son. He had been disabled through a fall aged 5, when news came of his father's and grandfather's deaths.[1] He had grown up in exile, unable to walk, having lost lands, title and rights. One can only imagine Mephibosheth's thoughts since and his apprehension on being summoned to David's presence.

Recognising his fear and his low self-opinion, David calls him repeatedly by name. For Jonathan's sake, David wants to show real kindness to the last of the family as he had promised. More than mere words, David's love will have significant consequences. Family lands will be restored, a retinue of labourers employed, and an income guaranteed. Fears quelled, Mephibosheth is offered an honoured place at the king's table, guaranteeing his acceptance and protection. The concepts of covenant kindness and a seat at the king's table due to the actions of a king's son have echoes for Christians today. We come to the Lord's table, symbol of the new covenant, because of what our King's Son, Jesus, has done for us and promised to us. We come at his invitation, not because we have a right to come.

What remains unclear is how Mephibosheth responded to such kindness. Clearly he took it, but was his heart changed as a result? That, for him and for us, is the crucial question.

Thank God for his kindness in including you in his family and inviting you to share with him at his table. Who could you show hospitality to?[2]

---

[1] 2 Sam 4:4 [2] Rom 12:13; Heb 13:2; 1 Pet 4:9,10

THINK WHAT YOU ARE DOING

Lord, we praise you today for your love shown in loyalty and your faithfulness shown in constant care.

2 SAMUEL 10

David seeks to repay a past kindness with an act of goodwill to the Ammonites, following the death of their king. However, his delegation is perceived as a scouting party rather than a diplomatic mission. The men are sent away humiliated. David, wanting to minimise their loss of face, allows them to withdraw to restore their dignity. Now, however, the Ammonites had to be dealt with. How foolish and short-sighted they were to provoke David to retaliate!

How easily we can be influenced by hotheads bent on their own agenda and how serious the results can be! Sometimes we rush into an unwise course of action without ever thinking through the consequences. There is no point in winning a battle if we are going to lose the war. The Ammonite adviser's fault was to impute, without evidence, unworthy motives to David. The result, for a moment of high defiance, was to be misery for all. We must be very careful whose advice we listen to. We need to recognise how significant our choice of advisers can be, for us and for others.

The resulting war forms the backdrop to the tragic events soon to unfold, involving David, Bathsheba and Uriah the Hittite. The action is described in brisk detail as the troops are gathered, mercenaries enrolled to swell the Ammonites' number, field positions taken and battle engaged. David's troops are ably led by Joab, a hardened commander, who drew up contingency plans for the forthcoming battle, prepared for any eventuality. As it happened the deployment of the enemy on two fronts backfired. Divided from each other, one half fled and was routed by David till they sued for peace. The other half barricaded themselves inside their city, Rabbah, round which Joab established a siege, prepared to wait for their eventual surrender.

How carefully do you think before giving advice to others? Have you got those you can trust to advise you?

WHAT ARE YOU DOING!

Lord, lead us not into temptation, but if we face it, show us a way of escape.[1]

2 SAMUEL 11:1–13

There is always a temptation to read into this story more than is recorded. There is so much we want to know about the relationship between David and Bathsheba. However, the aim of the writer is not to satisfy our voyeurism but to show in stark terms how power corrupts.

David changes his life pattern of leading from the front. Instead of finding the rest he seeks, he experiences a listlessness that leads to trouble when he spies a beautiful woman one evening. Used to command, he takes the initiative throughout this chapter, though he finds that not all events are under his control. He saw, he enquired, he sent for her, and then he slept with her. Ironically, the reason for her bathing, which aroused David's infatuation, had been to purify herself (v 4)! The narrative seems more filled with lust than love, and their brief encounter merely a one-night stand. The payback comes through her pregnancy; the only words that the woman (her name is rarely used) speaks are to report it. Still in charge, David seeks damage limitation by recalling Uriah, her husband, to report on the war. The very values he has instilled in his men of comradeship and solidarity, however, preclude Uriah from acting as David had expected and going home to Bathsheba. David tries again, using alcohol as a lubricant to weaken his resolve, but once again Uriah's default position prevents him from going home and David is thwarted for a second time.

We find it hard to recognise David in this chapter, but sense that a madness has gripped him. He is determined to do whatever it takes to conceal his adultery. He has lost all perspective and balance, and is getting deeper and deeper into trouble. How deceptive sin can be!

Are there areas of your life you are refusing to face up to, that are getting out of control? Let God's light shine on them before the shadows become deep darkness.[2]

[1] 1 Cor 10:13 [2] Jer 13:16,17; Ezek 18:30–32

HOW FAR WOULD YOU GO?

'Search me, O God, and know my heart today. / Try me, O Lord and know my thoughts I pray...'[1]

2 SAMUEL 11:14–27

What is it that makes us compound one wrong with another? As if adultery and an attempted cover-up were not enough, David now plans the execution of the man he has wronged. Furthermore, having failed to control Bathsheba's fertility, or undermine Uriah's loyalty, he unwisely now puts himself in the hands of Joab, his commander. Uriah's death is to look like a botched mission, not quite 'friendly fire' but heading that way. It seems almost inconsequential to David that in securing loyal Uriah's death others, too, would have to pay the ultimate price. Did he think to himself, 'Well, that's war, and you can't make an omelette without breaking eggs'? Is that the level to which David had descended? What a warning!

So Uriah the foreigner, who fought for David, died in battle, and a full report was sent by Joab. It was carried by a messenger who feared for the king's reaction to these casualty figures and the foolish military strategy that lay behind them. Cynically, Joab reassured him and encouraged him to name the fallen and in particular Uriah, and so he did. How did David feel at that moment – triumphant or empty? The deceit is played out in the comforting of the messenger and the vote of confidence in Joab!

We do not know how Bathsheba felt, nor how genuine was the official mourning. All we know is that once again David sent for her, this time to marry her before he took her to bed. A son was born – so game, set and match to David? No, not quite. After a chapter in which the deafening silence of God threatens to overwhelm, finally comes the only verdict that matters – the Lord's displeasure. All David's scheming has been observed by the only audience that counts. The day of reckoning lies ahead.

Thank God that he is not indifferent to our sin.

---

1 J Edwin Orr, 1912–87

CAUGHT RED-HANDED

We praise you, Lord, that even when we shut you out from our lives, you come knocking at the door.

2 SAMUEL 12:1–14

Nathan's forthright courage shines out again, this time accompanied with wisdom. He does not blunder in and denounce the king. Rather, he gets behind David's defences through telling a story. Here is a rich man who has everything – but who measures his life in 'things'. The poor man, in contrast, has little, yet he has a home life and even his lamb is a family pet. The inhumanity and greed of the rich man violating the life of the poor deeply angers the king. As judge, he pronounces sentence: the rich man's death would be justified.

'You are the man.' Just four words, and the carefully crafted web of deceit and self-justification is revealed for the empty, tawdry thing it always was. The Lord's ultimate desire is to restore David, but first he must face up to his wrongdoing and its consequences. David listens, his cheeks burning, as his actions are laid bare. There can be no justification for what he has done. God had been lavish in his generosity and would have given more if David had only asked, but David had been determined to have what he wanted and nobody, not even God, was going to get in the way. Murder is the first crime cited, then theft of Uriah's wife. Uriah's violent death will return to haunt David. Violence will mark the remainder of his reign, just when peace seems to have been secured. David had secretly invaded the sanctity of marriage, but his own marriage bed would be violated publicly and his wives degraded.

The final word is with David. His immediate confession is unqualified, with no attempt at justification. At last he is speaking to God again. But worse is to follow. He will not die, though he deserves to, but his baby son will. Sin is a serious matter.

'The Lord will not allow us to remain comfortable in sin but will ruthlessly expose it, lest we settle down in it.'[1]

---

[1] Dale Ralph Davis, *2 Samuel: Out of Every Adversity*, Focus on the Bible; Christian Focus, 1999

SIN LEAKS AND STAINS

'The fear of the LORD is the beginning of wisdom.'[1] 'Twas grace that taught my heart to fear, and grace my fears relieved.'[2]

2 SAMUEL 12:15–31

There is no protest by David. After all the 'sending' that David undertook in chapter 11, God had 'sent' Nathan to deliver his verdict. Now it began to be executed. The child became ill, and David turned to prayer. We do not know what was said, except that he pleaded for the child. The mercy he had failed to show to others was now drawn out of him, helpless before a tiny scrap of humanity. He would not be distracted or diverted from prayer by the offer of food or drink, or the encouragement to rest. Having restarted communication with God, there was a lot of catching up to do. The dam walls being broken, there was no stopping the flow.[3]

The death sentence was not commuted, however, and on the seventh day the child died. The household were frightened about the impact on the balance of their master's mind, but David received the news calmly and with resignation. He washed, worshipped and broke his fast. When asked for an explanation, all he would say was that while life remained he prayed, but now he could only trust to a reunion with his son beyond this life. The couple bound by tragedy and guilt sought comfort in each other. Bathsheba became pregnant and this time their son, Solomon, lived. There was no legacy from his brother's death and he was called 'loved by the LORD' or Jedidiah.

After nearly two years, the siege at Rabbah came to an end. David rode out to be there at the end to receive their surrender and negotiate terms for peace. The impact of that terrible period would remain for the rest of David's life. But though he would face many troubles in the years ahead, God was once again with him.

'You may succeed in unfaithfulness but the LORD will come after you, and that should comfort us.'[4]

---

[1] Prov 9:10   [2] From John Newton, 'Amazing Grace'   [3] See Ps 51   [4] Davis, *2 Samuel*

LOVELESS LOVE

'Love is as strong as death … It burns like blazing fire, like a mighty flame.'[1] Lord, deepen the fire of love within me today.

2 SAMUEL 13:1–22

The storyline is simple, memorable and painful: lust, deception, rape, abandonment. The last we hear of Tamar, who when summoned by Amnon and David acted dutifully, is that she is left 'a desolate woman' whose life has been ruined by Amnon's heartless brutality. As such she represents many down the ages whose lives have been shattered through no fault of their own, when beauty has evoked not love but lustful and malicious exploitation. Amnon, by contrast, is the embodiment of countless people whose reality has been memorably captured by Shakespeare: 'The expense of spirit in a waste of shame / Is lust in action … Enjoy'd no sooner but despised straight; / Past reason hunted; and, no sooner had, / Past reason hated …'[2]

It is curious that one and the same word, love, should indicate such different realities. I often wish that 'I am sexually attracted to' could be depicted by words other than 'I love'. For love, rightly understood (Paul's depiction[3] is famous) is an attitude, with related action, that seeks the well-being of another person. Yet sexual attraction is almost always, at least in part, a matter of self-seeking. Interestingly, however, the biblical writer uses 'love' in that same ambiguous and ambivalent sense that it has in English (vs 1,15), though the effect of such use in this narrative is to point up how unreliable the feeling of love is.

We may also note that David, although furious, does nothing. Why not? The text's silence makes us wonder. Many ancient manuscripts fill in the silence with an explanation that David did nothing because of 'love' for Amnon as his firstborn. Equally, however, David's adulterous and murderous love for Bathsheba would have diminished his moral authority over his family. Either way, David's misuse of love has left him feeling impotent to stop others following his example.

'Love is patient, love is kind … it is not self-seeking.'[4] Lord, teach me what true love is, and help me show it to others.

[1] Song 8:6 [2] Sonnet CXXIX [3] 1 Cor 13 [4] 1 Cor 13:4,5

STUPIDITY AND MALICE

'In regard to evil be infants, but in your thinking be adults.'[1] Lord, teach me more of your ways.

2 SAMUEL 13:23–39

It is difficult to decide which of the main characters in this narrative shows up in the worst light. David is stupid. To decline to go to Absalom's celebration was perfectly reasonable, and his initial refusal to send Amnon shows that he was suspicious of Absalom's request and could guess that something dubious was going on, but subsequently to give in to Absalom's urging shows him to be feeble and foolish, unable to act on his own convictions.

Jonadab is a man who pretends to be a helpful friend to others when in fact he is simply looking out for himself. Initially advising Amnon made sense, for Amnon was heir to the throne. Jonadab was the one who had put Amnon up to his abuse of Tamar – though he might have claimed that his advice only specified ogling and pampering (13:5), leaving it to Amnon to draw a further (implied) inference. Now Jonadab pops up again and coolly advises David that his sons are safe because Absalom's hatred was restricted to Amnon – which he, Jonadab, had long known. He also claims that the news that David's other sons are still alive means that everything has turned out 'just as your servant said' (v 35). One wonders whether Jonadab's accurate knowledge means that he was in on Absalom's plot too, and was now trying to use his knowledge to his own advantage.

Absalom clearly planned the murder carefully. A two-year time lag made it seem plausible he had got over his resentment towards Amnon. An out-of-town party would mean that Amnon would lack the servants and protection he would have back in the palace. Absalom then just had to outface his father, do the deed, and follow his father's example of fleeing to a neighbouring kingdom when home was too hot.[2]

Lord, may I never be misled by the appealing facade of sin. Keep me from temptations to take the easy or self-serving way out of difficult situations.

---

1 1 Cor 14:20 **2** Cf 1 Sam 21:10; 27:1–4

THE PRODIGAL SON – NOT

'The tongue is a small part of the body, but it makes great boasts.'[1] Lord, use my tongue today to speak for your glory and to sing your praises.

2 SAMUEL 14:1–22

Joab was David's 'chief of staff' and also his 'fixer'; entirely loyal, but by his own lights. Joab did what he reckoned needed to be done for David, whether or not David approved: he murdered Abner, for example.[2] However much David complained, he never reined in Joab – until Joab killed Absalom, when David replaced him with Amasa; when Joab subsequently murdered Amasa he got his job back again.[3] Joab was clearly a hard man and a force to be reckoned with. He is the prime mover in today's account of David's recall of his estranged son; for Joab had decided that a reconciliation between David and Absalom was in David's interests – though he presumably came to regret this decision. He may have learned from Nathan that David was open to picture and parable where more direct speech might have failed.[4] So he primes a 'wise woman' (v 2) to get through to the king, under the guise of a case of dispute.[5]

The woman produces a story with certain analogies to David's situation. Although it is hard to catch the tone of the dialogue, the woman clearly wants more than a routine assurance from David and so persists until David commits himself with an oath. She then applies her story to David's refusal to pardon Absalom. David instantly senses that the woman would not do this unless put up to it, and so asks about Joab, the one he knows to be most likely to try such a tactic. When the woman comes clean, David acquiesces. Joab then shrewdly speaks of his doing David a favour (as he thinks) as though David is doing him a favour. It is a sophisticated negotiation. Yet it leaves out issues of forgiveness and repentance – an omission which will come back with a vengeance.

Lord, help me to honour you with wise and truthful speech.

---

[1] James 3:5   [2] 2 Sam 3:19–39   [3] *See* 2 Sam 19:13; 20:9,10,23   [4] *Cf* 2 Sam 12:1–7   [5] *Cf* 2 Sam 15:4; 1 Kings 3:16–28

BEAUTY AND THE BEAST

'You have made us for yourself, and our hearts are restless till they find their rest in you.'[1] Thank you, Lord, for the wonder of being your creation.

David's relationship with Absalom is clearly complex. His soft spot for Absalom, which Joab had discerned, remained potent even when Absalom led a rebellion.[2] Nonetheless, for some reason (ambivalent anger?) he cannot bring himself to summon Absalom to his presence for (at least) a formal reconciliation. Presumably the lack of such formal reconciliation meant that Absalom in 'his own house' (v 24) was under some kind of house arrest which prevented him from resuming normal life within Jerusalem; hence Absalom's frustration.

The narrator pauses, however, to speak of Absalom's exceptionally good looks. Why? Perhaps to suggest, in anticipation, one element in the attraction that Absalom had for the people of Israel, who were soon to rally to him. The mention of his hair prepares us for the grisly fate that Absalom eventually met[3] – though Absalom's weighing of his hair also tacitly suggests that he sets great store by his appearance. Absalom's character, however, does not match his good looks. He gets frustrated with his father for not seeing him, and frustrated with Joab for not 'fixing' it. When Joab adds insult to injury by not even responding to his summons, Absalom decides to communicate in the kind of language he knows best – brutish aggression, in the form of destruction of property. This certainly has its desired effect in getting Joab to do what he wants and, sure enough, to 'fix' his formal reconciliation with his father. Since, however, the next time that we hear of Joab and Absalom being together Joab runs a helpless Absalom through with spears,[4] one imagines that Joab did not appreciate his mode of summons and was happy to get his own back, with interest. Both Absalom and Joab are macho men, who prefer to act like animals rather than beings created in the image of God.

Lord, help me to look beyond outward appearances and to reflect your image in the way I live my life today.

[1] Augustine of Hippo, 354–430 [2] *See* 2 Sam 18:5,33 [3] 2 Sam 18:9 [4] 2 Sam 18:14

RELIGIOUS TRICKERY

'The fruit of the Spirit is ... goodness.'[1] Thank you, Lord, for the gift of life in all its fullness.

2 SAMUEL 15:1–12

Some things seem to change very little. Still today politicians who aspire for office make all sorts of promises to people that they will give them what they really want, and generally try to make themselves as accessible and winsome as possible. So too Absalom, who has to get a popular following if he is to displace his father. The ancient equivalent of the presidential limousine and outriders is also there, in the chariot and men running ahead. A concern with image is no modern innovation but is as old as the unregenerate heart.

Interestingly, we are never told why Absalom decides to set himself up against his father. Maybe he was impatient. Being heir to the throne was not enough – David was 'past it' and Absalom wanted things now. At any event, David does indeed seem to have lost his grip. Instead of making sure he knows what is going on, he seems oblivious to the fact that Absalom is deliberately setting himself up for a kingly role (administering justice) and displacing his father in popular sentiment. He seems to have no suspicion that Absalom's request to go to Hebron might be other than it appeared to be.

For his part, Absalom knows that the best way to appear innocent is to appear pious. Absalom presents himself as someone who makes vows to the Lord, and who takes them seriously; fulfilling the vow must involve not only an act of worship but a formal ceremony with invited guests (including the esteemed political pundit, Ahithophel). There is nothing second-rate or on the cheap when Absalom worships God. Although religious language and apparent piety do not go down well in contemporary Britain, they still bring substantial political leverage in other parts of the world; voters will do well not to be credulous.

'Search me, God, and know my heart.'[2] Lord, keep me from hypocrisy. May all that I say and do today be genuine.

---

[1] Gal 5:22 [2] Ps 139:23

RUN FOR YOUR LIFE

**'Oh, praise the greatness of our God! He is the Rock ... a faithful God.'[1]
Lord, thank you for your wonderful faithfulness, today and every day.**

2 SAMUEL 15:13–37

Whether or not David's decision to flee from Jerusalem was the right one we do not know. It might have been a poor decision, making him more vulnerable. One wonders why the voice of Joab receives no mention. Anyway, once the decision is made, everything turns to the practical arrangements that it entails.

David's approach is reminiscent of Oliver Cromwell's attitude, that one should 'trust God and keep one's powder dry'. The emphasis of the narrative, however, is more upon keeping the powder dry than upon trusting God. David here is like his ancestor Jacob when Jacob was preparing for a life-or-death encounter with his brother Esau:[2] he prays, but he calculates more. David's spiritual stature here appears less than in his earlier life. His words with Zadok indeed mention the Lord's favour but can quite naturally be read rather fatalistically – there is no urgent seeking of the Lord's face here – and as a way of rationalising his preference to have Zadok and his family remain in Jerusalem to be David's eyes and ears there. Likewise, although David's prayer about Ahithophel appears to be from the heart (v 31),and indeed is going to be answered by the Lord,[3] the narrator's emphasis falls more upon David's instructions to Hushai to be the human agent for frustrating Ahithophel and also cooperating with Zadok and his family.

David's dialogue with Ittai – who comes from Gath, and is therefore a Philistine – is striking in a different way. His reasons for Ittai not to accompany him are good ones, yet Ittai responds with a profession of life-and-death loyalty that places him alongside Ruth, another foreigner from another historic enemy of Israel.[4] Jesus later pointed out the same shaming paradox, that loyalty and faithful responsiveness may be greater outside the realm of God's chosen people than within it.[5]

Lord, keep me faithful to you and your church, come what may.

[1] Deut 32:3,4 [2] Gen 32:3–21 [3] 2 Sam 17:14 [4] Ruth 1:16,17 [5] Matt 8:10

PROFITEERING

'You know the grace of our Lord Jesus Christ, that though he was rich, yet for your sake he became poor.'[1] Thank you, Lord, for giving yourself for me.

2 SAMUEL 16:1–14

Ziba and Shimei, representatives of the displaced house of King Saul, see David's unprecedented weakness as their opportunity. One of the perennial problems when public order breaks down is that the unscrupulous see the difficulties as their chance to enrich themselves at others' expense. Ziba is no exception, even though he initially appears to be a generous provider for David. When in verse 3 David points out (in effect) that all these gifts weren't his to provide, Ziba suggests that his master, Mephibosheth, son of David's friend Jonathan,[2] is disloyal to David and that he, Ziba, is loyally taking matters into his own hands – for which David amply rewards him.

It is very likely, however, that Ziba is lying, so as to enrich himself at Mephibosheth's expense. The claim that Mephibosheth thought he would regain the kingdom is ludicrous: why should Absalom go to so much trouble to gain the kingdom only to give it away to a cripple with none of Absalom's public attractiveness and to whom he owed nothing? Indeed, the fact that Mephibosheth had been so generously provided for by David was probably what made Ziba gamble that David was worth backing; for if Absalom took over, all that Mephibosheth had enjoyed would be lost. Moreover, Mephibosheth's subsequent defence of his failure to join David[3] – that Ziba stole his only means of transport – rings true, both because of his mourning during David's absence and because of his willingness to concede his goods to Ziba, analogous to the truthful prostitute before Solomon.[4]

In the circumstances, David had little choice but to accept and make use of Ziba's provision. Nonetheless, his granting of all Mephibosheth's estate to Ziba is clearly premature, a sign that he is no longer exercising the kind of discernment needed by a king/judge.

Lord, help me to be wise and discerning about whom I trust; and grant that I may never use another's misfortune for my gain.

[1] 2 Cor 8:9   [2] See 2 Sam 9   [3] 2 Sam 19:24–30   [4] 1 Kings 3:26,27

DISHONEST FOR GOD?

'We know that in all things God works for the good of those who love him.'[1] Thank you, Lord, for this wonderful truth.

2 SAMUEL 16:15 – 17:14

To be an undercover agent must be one of life's least desirable roles. One's own future, and that of one's sponsor, depend on one's ability to speak and act dishonestly. Whatever the thrills of spy stories, the reality, however successful the agent, will always be deeply tainted, a painful testimony to life in a fallen world. Hushai's initial encounter with Absalom well demonstrates his understanding of what to do to appear plausible. Not least, like Absalom earlier, Hushai knows that a lie can go down better if backed by a pious appeal to God's will (v 18).

Ahithophel's initial advice may appear puzzling: why bother with the concubines when there were other, apparently more pressing, matters for Absalom to attend to (although of course this fulfils Nathan's earlier pronouncement of judgement on David)?[2] However, the action has heavy symbolic significance: sex with a royal concubine could appear to be equivalent to claiming the place of king.[3] Elsewhere, Reuben's lying with his father Jacob's concubine, and the consequent curse, shows that this is a symbolic burning of bridges.[4] We should spare a thought for the concubines who, like Tamar earlier, have a dismal existence as the objects of male sexual politics – as do many young women sold into sex slavery today, only worse.[5]

The conflicting counsels of Ahithophel and Hushai are fascinating. Knowing of David's disheartened condition, we have no difficulty recognising Ahithophel's advice as apposite. But Hushai's graphic scenario is fully plausible. Ahithophel had not spoken foolishly, as David had prayed,[6] but his good counsel is ignored, which amounts to the same thing. Given Ahithophel's excellent reputation, Absalom erred in wanting to consult Hushai in the first place. Whatever his motives, the Lord overruled them to preserve his chosen king.

Lord, help me to recognise when faithfulness means choosing a lesser evil.

[1] Rom 8:28 [2] 2 Sam 12:11,12 [3] *Cf* 2 Sam 3:7; 1 Kings 1:1–15; 2:17,22 [4] *See* Gen 35:22; 49:3,4 [5] *See* www.chaste.org.uk [6] 2 Sam 15:31

RELIEF AND DESPAIR

'You exalted me above my foes ... therefore I will praise you, LORD, among the nations.'[1] Thank you, Lord, for the joy of knowing you and being rescued by you.

2 SAMUEL 17:15–29

Hushai knows that Absalom has decided to follow his counsel but is still nervous lest he should change his mind, so he has to get a warning message to David from occupied Jerusalem. The action is of a kind familiar from many a story of war and occupied territory: an insignificant person, a servant girl, is chosen to be a go-between; the couriers are spotted and have to hide; a family conceal them and lie appropriately to the search party; there is eventually a successful getaway and the message is delivered, which enables David to escape across the Jordan to safety. Once there, David and his men are given generous hospitality and refreshment, all the more welcome because it would have symbolised safety and a home from home. Although Absalom's army must still be confronted, there seems to be little sense of doubt that David's followers, once suitably refreshed and reinforced, will be likely to do well in battle. The Lord has delivered David – though there is no mention of David giving thanks or finding strength in the Lord, as he did on other occasions.[2]

Ahithophel must have been an old man, for he was grandfather to David's latest wife, Bathsheba.[3] Presumably he is not simply miffed that Hushai's counsel was preferred to his, but he also realises that Absalom's best chance of securing his position has gone and that David may well win on the rebound. After his opportunistic disloyalty to his family,[4] he reckons there will be no future for him if Absalom fails, and not a long future even if Absalom wins. So, correctly judging the likely outcome of events, he decides not to wait around while things unravel. Sadly, he dies as he had recently lived, in a world made up of success and failure, of esteem and shame and despair – a world without repentance, forgiveness or hope of mercy.

Lord, never let my heart grow cold, and never let me lose sight of your world of faith, hope and love.

[1] 2 Sam 22:49,50 [2] eg 1 Sam 30:6; 2 Sam 22; Ps 18 [3] *See* 2 Sam 11:3; 23:34 [4] 2 Samuel 15:12

A MAN OF GOD?

'The LORD is our God, bringing justice everywhere on earth... Shout praises to the LORD!'[1]

2 SAMUEL 18:1–18

At one level, Absalom caused David nothing but trouble. He was like a cabinet minister or military commander who is out of control. He should have been dismissed from the cabinet or exiled. First, Absalom killed one of David's sons, Amnon, having harboured deep hatred against him for two years because he had abused Tamar, Absalom's sister. Absalom then fled and was restored to David through another cunning plot engineered by Joab, David's army commander. Then he plotted discontent in David's kingdom, appealing particularly to the northern tribes. Eventually, he was liked better than David and managed to get to Hebron – the one-time capital – and gathered an army. David was so fearful that Absalom would succeed that he fled Jerusalem. His fears were well founded, because Absalom was pronounced king on his arrival. Yet in spite of all this vicious trouble which Absalom had caused, David still loved him as one of his sons.

From a military and political point of view this was weakness and folly. So Joab can be seen as acting in David's best interests when he ensured that Absalom was brutally killed off (vs 14,15) – but Joab had his own reasons for wanting Absalom out of the way. Not only had Absalom affronted Joab by setting his barley field on fire,[2] but Joab probably resented the attention David gave to Absalom and saw him as a threat to his position as David's chief of staff. David knew this and did all he could to protect Absalom from Joab's intentions, by publicly issuing a 'protection order' for Absalom, but it made no difference to Joab. In the end Joab was not loyal and supportive to David; he thought he knew best and should take decisions over David's head and certainly against David's heart. Are we sometimes like him?

Father God, help me to act justly and lovingly when I am faced with confusing and morally ambivalent situations at work and in my family.

[1] Ps 105:7,45, CEV [2] 2 Sam 14:30

A DOUBLE CONTEST

'Please listen, LORD God, and answer my prayers. Make my eyes sparkle again.'[1]

2 SAMUEL 18:19–33

People take part in the London Marathon for all kinds of reasons: a few run to win; many to prove they can do it and raise money for charity. Often those who win this and similar races are from Ethiopia. Ethiopia has a long history of great runners, and we meet one here – a Cushite. Yet he meets his match: Ahimaaz, son of Zadok the priest, outruns him. Winning seems more important to them than their news that David's son Absalom has been brutally murdered. Looked at in this way, their competitive spirit is selfish and damaging. They challenge us to consider whether, in our endeavours to succeed – getting the best stereo system, car, garden, house, degree, promotion, status or even a role in church – we are overlooking far more fundamental issues. Are we damaging our children or our relationships, including marriage, because we are too competitive? Are we neglecting to develop our compassion because we so want to succeed?

But why all this time spent on a race? In one sense it simply delays the inevitable – that moment in the story when David will understand the dreadful truth that Absalom is dead. It increases our anxiety for David and so encourages us to share in his overwhelming grief more deeply. His simple words draw us to tears: 'My son, Absalom! My son, my son Absalom! I wish I could have died instead of you! Absalom, my son, my son!' (v 33, CEV).

More profoundly, this 'narrative technique' mirrors the reality. Underneath both the race and the death of Absalom are the same story – of the damage caused by human pride and ambition. Absalom competes with David for the kingship, and with Joab for the king's favour, behaviour which leads to this gruesome tragedy.

Father God, help me to run well, but always with my eyes fixed on Jesus, knowing that my faith depends on him[2] and that my character should reflect his.[3]

[1] Ps 13:3, CEV [2] Heb 12:2 [3] 2 Cor 3:18

THE SHOW MUST GO ON

'Protect me, LORD God! I run to you for safety, and I have said, "Only you are my Lord!"'[1]

2 SAMUEL 19:1–15a

We have grown used to – and perhaps some of the time even enjoy – the invasion of the private lives of public figures, both celebrities and politicians. This passage of scripture reminds us that even royals are human beings. David could not hide his deep grief, the anguish of a father on the abrupt death of his son, brutally murdered. David's grief was probably intensified by the fact that there had been such a deep rift between himself and Absalom, and that they had spent many years apart.

While most of us will not be dealing with royalty or celebrities, we do well to remember that the 'public figures' whom we do know are also real people. The minister, the bishop, the teacher who is responsible for our children, the people at work – they all have deep emotions. So too do the receptionist, the cleaner, the checkout assistant and, yes, even the traffic warden! If you find the bullying tactics of Joab abhorrent, then please remember that the 'public' people you meet today may well be suffering. Perhaps they are in physical pain or their young child has kept them awake all night and they are worried for them. They may be facing financial debt, ill health or the fallout from a broken relationship – all forms of suffering that you and I may never be aware of. While it is true that Joab trampled on David's feelings deliberately and we may claim ignorance as an excuse, this passage prompts reflection on our attitudes towards people in public life; how generous and caring are we towards them?

Of course, there is another side to this story – Joab was concerned that the business of establishing law and order should not be neglected. Balancing private grief with public office is never easy.

Father God, help me, with the grief, anxiety and guilt I carry, still to live graciously and effectively for your kingdom.

---

[1] Ps 16:1,2, CEV

SETTLING OLD SCORES

'With all my heart I praise the LORD! ... I will never forget how kind he has been. The LORD forgives our sins.'[1]

2 SAMUEL 19:15b–30

Verses 9-14 provide the context for the cameos in today's verses. David had fled Jerusalem when Absalom rebelled. Many there supported Absalom - what position did that leave them in now? Would David attack Jerusalem and show who was boss? These verses show how David offered an olive branch to the worried leaders in Jerusalem - he encouraged them to invite him back, thus providing the whole city with a way to avoid punishment. They were glad to respond. But how did that leave those individuals who had taken a significant part in the rebellion?

Today's reading shows that David extended forgiveness and renewed acceptance to people like Shimei and Mephibosheth who had supported Absalom either openly or complicitly. Why did he grant a complete pardon to Shimei and only a conditional one to Mephibosheth? It seems that Shimei was open about his fault and truly repentant, whereas Mephibosheth made excuses. David's forgiving spirit looked like weakness to some of his followers. There was a case for saying that if only David had quashed Absalom firmly earlier on, probably killing him at an early sign of his rebellion, all this trouble would not have happened. So Abishai shouts at Shimei: 'You should be killed for cursing the LORD's chosen king!' (v 21, CEV).

It was as though he wanted to underline the seriousness of what Shimei had done and encourage David to think again. But David will show mercy to whom he chooses and he chooses to show it to all. Joab and Abishai should remember who is king! Here, if nowhere else, David shows that he is a man after God's own heart. He forgives his enemies and protects them from the wrath of his friends, while challenging his followers to live a life of compassion and generosity.

David withstood the norms requiring punishment, showing kindness. How can we do the same? Pray that we may have the strength of Christ.

---

1 Ps 103:1–3a, CEV

GROWING OLD GRACEFULLY

'I will praise you, LORD God, for your mighty deeds and your power to save. You have taught me since I was a child ... Don't leave me when I am old.'[1]

2 SAMUEL 19:31–43

This final encounter is beautiful. Here we see David dealing gently with an old man, Barzillai. In David's hour of desperation Barzillai had provided for him, and by so doing risked incurring death at the hands of Absalom.[2] David wanted to reward this man for his generosity, but initially overlooked his fragility. Once alerted to it, he responded with understanding and sensitivity. Like the one who was to come, he would not damage a bruised reed.[3]

David's sympathetic response challenges us all to understand older people's situations. Barzillai's explanation helpfully makes the situation of older people clear; his approach is a challenge to all who are older. Political prestige gained by accompanying the triumphant king no longer counted. All the luxuries and pampering that could be his, alongside the king, would mean nothing to him as his 'body is almost numb' (v 35). Like many older people, he senses that he could be a 'burden' (v 35). Because he could not join enthusiastically in the partying, people might mute their own celebrations or think that he disapproved. If Barzillai thought he was spoiling others' enjoyment, that would upset him even more. All he really wanted was to return to his home, where he felt secure because of all the familiarity – a place which enriched his waning senses because it was full of the most significant and fragrant of memories. One day soon he would be buried alongside his own parents! Given all of this, how courageous and generous he is to offer to David his servant. To let him go meant losing the support and friendship of one who truly understood him and knew how best to care for him physically and emotionally. Yet he wanted to give this servant the opportunity to receive the benefits that David was offering him.

David's and Barzillai's behaviour challenges us. How do we treat older people? As older people, do we release others, even when it is costly?

[1] Ps 71:16–18a, CEV [2] 2 Sam 17:27–29 [3] Isa 42:3, NIV

HARSH REALITIES!

'From a sea of troubles I call out to you, LORD. Won't you please listen as I beg for mercy?'[1]

2 SAMUEL 20

After the sensitivity of the previous passage, this one faces us with the harsh realities of tribal life. We read of two people's deaths, but for very different reasons. David would have wanted neither killing, but he was implicated in both. Ultimately, both have their roots in his adultery with Bathsheba. One of the purposes of the unfolding story of David's kingship in 2 Samuel is to trace the impact of sin. We should reflect on the way our (communal and personal) sinful choices cause death around the world: consumerism and global warming, and protecting our security with violence, for instance.

Amasa is killed by Joab because of Joab's vicious jealousy and lust for power. Joab had killed Absalom, David's son, in clear and stark disobedience to David's instructions, even though he knew how deeply Absalom's death would wound David.[2] Probably in view of this, David appoints Amasa (rather than Joab) to gather and then lead the troops commissioned to put down Sheba's rebellion. Joab stabs Amasa even as he shakes hands with him. Then, to underline the brutality of the age, because the troops pursuing Sheba are distracted as they pause to view the dying Amasa, a soldier drags him out of sight and leaves him there.

The other person to die is the leader of the rebellion, Sheba. He meets his end through the subterfuge of the wise woman of the city, where he and his army had taken refuge. She negotiates with Joab to spare the city if Sheba is handed over. Joab is happy to agree. So, Sheba is handed over – or at least his severed head is. As someone was to remark a millennium later – it is better that one man die rather than all the people.[3]

Reflect carefully on the psalmist's words: 'If you kept record of our sins, no one could last long.'[4] Then read the next verse!

---

[1] Ps 130:1,2 [2] 2 Sam 18 [3] Caiaphas; *see* John 11:50 [4] Ps 130:3, CEV

DAVID THE NEGOTIATOR

'In my distress I called upon the LORD; to my God I called ... and my cry came to his ears.'[1]

The people had survived two years of drought and famine. David sought the Lord and realised that the root problem was an injustice committed against the Gibeonites, and he set out to put it right. The problem went back to the settlement of the land, when the Gibeonites' fear led to deception, and to Joshua's promise to protect them.[2] In return they were forced into bonded labour, but Saul had resented this pagan presence and eventually had many of them killed.

Legacies of injustice have always been part of our world – African slaves, Bosnian Muslims, German Jews, Iraqi Christians. Even in ordinary everyday life there are unfair dismissals, false accusations, unjust favouritism. I remember a family of several children that included a foster son. Divisive resentment became so difficult that the foster child was taken back into care. The family's sense of failure at betraying a trust was hard for them to bear.

David had to work out how to handle the problem. How do we deal with difficult entrenched situations? David's first move was to acknowledge the grievance and listen to the Gibeonites, asking them for their solution. But the solution they offered gave David a terrible task. Maybe it was only seven lives sacrificed for hundreds dead and years of misery, but the law said that sons should not pay the penalty for their fathers' sins.[3] David broke his promise to protect Saul's family, just as Saul had broken a promise to protect the Gibeonites.

So the executions happened, and the dead bodies were hung up for all to see (impaling being probably the exposure of the dead, not the form of execution), to show that expiation had been made. David then brought closure by an act of gentle finality, honouring Saul and his kin and honouring Rizbah and her devoted vigil. Then the rains came.

Lord, help us to face up to any injustices in our relationships at home, work or community – and in our wider world, however difficult.

[1] 2 Sam 22:7, NRSV [2] Josh 9:3–27 [3] Deut 24:16; *see also* Ezek 18:20

THE WEARY COMMANDER

'Come to me, all you that are weary ... and I will give you rest. Take my yoke upon you, and learn from me; for I am gentle and humble in heart.'[1]

2 SAMUEL 21:15–22

I suppose we all feel a sense of loss when we lose physical strength and ability, but for strong successful people it can be particularly hard. David the warrior king, the shepherd who fought for his sheep, who probably disliked staying at home with the paperwork, became weary, and men whom he led had to take over. They killed the giants he could no longer kill, and they told him to go home and run the country. The exploits and adventures were no longer for him. 'Saul has slain his thousands, and David his tens of thousands',[2] the people had sung as the army returned triumphant, when David was young. Now, at the end of his reign, he would be the negotiator, the diplomat, the planner – essential work, but work that probably attracted argument and quibble rather than heroic song.

David was 'the lamp of Israel' (v 17). They couldn't do without him. He must not wear himself out in physically demanding and dangerous battles. Did he feel loss as he walked away from the battlefield and from the high-profile exploits of a commander-in-chief? Perhaps it was here, in the giving up of prestige and glory, that David reminds us of Jesus, great David's greater son, who also knew weariness, thirst and disappointment.

We learn from this that even the strongest become weak at times, and it is the way we deal with weakness that counts. When Paul was weak the Lord said to him, 'My grace is sufficient for you, for power is made perfect in weakness.' So Paul could say, 'I will boast all the more gladly of my weaknesses, so that the power of Christ may dwell in me.'[3]

Lord, help me to accept it when there are things I can no longer do well. Help me to be willing to let others take over from me. May I boast in my weakness so that Christ's power may dwell in me.

---

[1] Matt 11:28 [2] 1 Sam 18:7 [3] 2 Cor 12:9, NRSV

DAVID THE PRAISE-SINGER

Help us, Lord, to remember what you have done and praise you with our lives, not just our lips.

This song[1] was written after David was anointed by Samuel,[2] after he had survived Saul's attempts on his life, and perhaps when he first became king, sure of the Lord's power to deliver all his promises. Could he still sing it with the same certainty at the end of his life and reign? Do we look back and remember when we sang with total abandon, sure of our relationship with the Lord, thrilled to give him our lives and knowing that we would do great deeds in his strength? Sometimes that first certainty and joy loses its freshness, leaving a sense of regret about the way things have turned out.

As we read this psalm it would help to remember two things. First, this song of praise may well have been sung as part of the people's worship during David's reign, just as it has been through the Christian centuries. It is the public 'property' of the people of God. But it is also the intimate, personal prayer of one man, inspired by the Holy Spirit to give us, from his own experience, a life-transforming picture of the power of God to save us, and keep on saving us, till we meet him face to face.

David begins with a passionate focus on God's power – rock, fortress, shield, saviour. These are not impersonal attributes, however: he is my rock, my saviour, and when I call he hears me and saves me. And his power to save is as great as his power in creation (vs 8–16) and certainly great enough to rescue anyone from any depth (vs 5,6). We may find it easy to sing such words, getting caught up in the passion of David's poetry, But do I really believe that God is this powerful and can rescue me where I am now?

We thank you, Lord, for the emotional power in poetry and music, especially when we sing together. Help us to take that joy and heartfelt praise into our daily lives.

---

[1] Almost identical to Ps 18 [2] 1 Sam 16:11–13

DAVID THE RIGHTEOUS?

'Search me, O God, and know my heart; test me and know my anxious thoughts. See if there is any wicked way in me, and lead me in the way everlasting.'[1]

2 SAMUEL 22:17–30

From an emphasis on the power of God, David turns to the joy of rescue and salvation. God reached for me, took me, drew me, delivered me and above all, delighted in me. But how do we read verses 21–25? Is this youthful arrogance, or is it, perhaps, a reference to David's refusal to harm Saul, even when Saul was aiming to destroy him? Could we pray using these words: 'The Lord rewarded me according to my righteousness. I have been blameless before you'?

David also acknowledges that the humble are saved, the proud and haughty brought low (v 28). So maybe he knew that he should not boast that he was blameless, but was recognising that obedience to God's commands is required of all his servants, all the time. This may be David in his confident youth, yet we know that he learnt from bitter experience just how badly even the best can fail and sin.[2] Then he had to throw himself on the mercy of God and find full forgiveness.[3] He learnt that we keep ourselves blameless, not in our own strength, but through the Lord's love and transforming power and in daily seeking his forgiveness and cleansing. He could still sing this song as his life drew to a close.

David didn't know the full glory that would be revealed in Jesus Christ his descendant, who would be King for ever, and who would fulfil all the covenant promises of God. As disciples of Jesus Christ, we know the cost of the righteousness that is ours by faith. With Paul, we can say, 'I regard [all things] garbage, that I may gain Christ and be found in him, not having a righteousness of my own that comes from the law, but that which is through faith in Christ.'[4]

We cannot see the future nor fully evaluate the past. We trust God and sing this song for ourselves in faith, clothed in his righteousness.

---

[1] Ps 139:23,24, NIV [2] 2 Sam 11:26 – 12:15 [3] *See* especially Ps 51 [4] Phil 3:8,9

DAVID THE VICTOR

'Be strong in the Lord ... For our struggle is not against enemies of blood and flesh, but against the ... spiritual forces of evil.'[1]

2 SAMUEL 22:31–51

In my circle of friends, there have been a number of 'battles': someone with a badly damaged knee that has changed her life drastically; a couple who were childless for many years – but when they had given up and were at the end of all possibilities produced a son and then twin girls; a man who recently was made redundant and then discovered he had a serious heart problem; a friend who finds praying very difficult.

At the beginning of 1 Samuel, Hannah prayed a 'song' to the Lord, when he had given her a longed-for child, Samuel. Her song is very similar to David's, here at the end of 2 Samuel. She ended with the words: 'The LORD ... will give strength to his king, and exalt the power of his anointed,'[2] words echoed by David (v 51). These two servants of the Lord, an ordinary woman and the king, had fought very different battles. But each of them knew that the battles they had won had been won through the Lord, their rock, who had girded them with strength, trained their hands, and demonstrated his steadfast love.

David's song is a song of triumph in the victories he has won through the Lord. God has been part of everything he has achieved. But his song is also a challenge to him – and to us. He knew and we know that his life had not been all triumph. There had been great loss, personal anguish, deliberate sin, procrastination and neglect of duty, poor relationships and betrayal. Maybe David in his youth knew he needed God's support when he went into battle against flesh and blood armies – but did he seek the Lord's strength for the everyday battles against the spiritual forces that sought to defeat him?

We all have battles – at work, in relationships, with stress and busyness, with temptation. We need the whole armour of God, to fight and stand firm. Pray through Ephesians 6:10–17.

[1] Eph 6:10,12, NRSV [2] 1 Sam 2:10b, NRSV; *cf* Matt 6:10

DAVID THE PROPHET

'Your kingdom come. Your will be done, on earth as it is in heaven.'[1]

2 SAMUEL 23:1–7

What's your idea of a perfect place? David pictures a perfect moment – dawn on a cloudless day, the grass lush and green from the rain. In temperate northern Europe we may not fully appreciate the joy of rain-soaked vegetation, but the people of Israel knew the joy of rain and the fertility it brought. They could say, 'The boundary lines have fallen for me in pleasant places; I have a goodly heritage.'[2] It is wonderful to be able to say, 'My world is a pleasant place', but in many parts of the world, that is seldom true. In refugee camps, in the slums of huge cities, in places of famine and drought, war and unrest, life is not pleasant.

David hints at some of the conditions needed for a pleasant, beautiful and fertile world: good government, justice, the recognition of God's laws, particularly in our care for the environment, order and security for the people. David's kingdom, united and at peace, was for a time a pleasant place. This oracle, David's 'last words', given to him by the Lord, is for his descendants who will rule after him. Rule justly, he tells them, let there be order and security; pursue the prosperity that comes from seeking the Lord's help and desiring to obey his law. Then, as he has promised, the Lord will give peace, prosperity and a throne that is secure for ever.

Perhaps this oracle of David from God was one of the great documents of the kingdom. Did Solomon know it, when he ended his reign building altars to the bloodthirsty gods of his pagan wives? Or did his son, Rehoboam, who burdened the people with hard service and brutal discipline? These were some of the godless ones, who betrayed the kingdom into the hands of the enemy, leading to destruction and exile.

When we pray 'your kingdom come', help us to see how we need to play our part in securing your kingdom, a pleasant place, in our homes, communities and world.

[1] Matt 6:10 [2] Ps 16:6, NRSV

DAVID THE BELOVED

'We know love by this, that he laid down his life for us – and we ought to lay down our lives for one another.'[1]

2 SAMUEL 23:8–39

Every November in churches and by war memorials we remember those who have died in the wars of the twentieth and twenty-first centuries. It is sobering: too often we see on our televisions the desolate misery of those who have lost loved ones. In these verses we have a list of the soldiers who served under David to protect the people of God. We also hear some of the incidents and stories that were told around camp fires and back home – the lion killed on the day it snowed, the fight in a field of lentils – and then, right at the end, Uriah the Hittite, betrayed by his captain and his king. Was that story told? Did Solomon know how David had acquired his mother? Some miseries are hard to live with.

Then there is the story of three men on a daring adventure. They won't get a medal for bringing back a drink of water from behind the enemy lines! In fact, they could probably be court-martialled for unnecessary risk, endangering lives and provoking an enemy attack. But it is a great story: David's longing for his captured home, the soldiers' love for him, and a successful adventure. He cannot drink the water won through such risk, so he pours it out as an offering, giving back to God their love and sacrifice.

Once, for a project, I read the diaries and letters of men who fought in the First World War. In the close relationships of the battlefield, in trenches and tanks, they found a deep love for each other, reciprocal sharing and sacrifice that they had never known before, not in their marriages or their communities. Some of them found return to civilian life profoundly difficult. Was it like that for David and his men?

What kind of love do we offer to our families, friends, fellow Christians? Do we forget to phone, have no time? How can we create fellowships where we love each other as the Lord has loved us?

---

[1] 1 John 3:16, NRSV

DAVID TEMPTED

'If you will not obey me ... I will break your proud glory ... your strength shall be spent to no purpose: your land shall not yield its produce.'[1]

2 SAMUEL 24:1–17

Where is God in this? What kind of a God can let this happen? Whenever there is a disaster, some people ask these questions. If we had only this chapter, how would we picture God? He became angry at something the people were doing, so he 'incited' David to sin by counting them, and then he sent an angel to spread a plague as punishment. (Interestingly, the same story is told in Chronicles, where it is Satan, the accuser, who 'incites' David.[2]) But, of course, we don't have just this chapter to tell us what God is like. We need to read all the Old Testament narratives in the light of the whole of Scripture. Then we understand a little of what the loving discipline of the Lord might involve.

In the same way that God allowed the accuser to tempt Job, he allowed David to be tempted. If Joab knew this was wrong, then so did David, but the people were restless, war might come at any time and he wanted to know how many potential soldiers he could rely on. This contradicted his own words that he should rely on God's power to win battles, not on the size of his army. Poor Joab was out for nine months to no good purpose!

David had to learn his lesson and the people had to learn theirs. The Lord had warned them that when the land became peaceful and prosperous they would turn away from him in pride and self-sufficiency. David repented, but forgiveness came at a cost. The people had sinned too, and Gad brought David a choice. He was the king. He had to take responsibility for the consequences, although he cried out in anguish at the cost (v 17). The continuation of this story shows that God is still working out his purposes through David and through Israel, even in these puzzling and tragic events.

God's justice and love, mercy and forgiveness do not necessarily take away the consequences of sin. Sometimes we have to trust where we cannot understand.

[1] Lev 26:14,19,20, NRSV [2] 1 Chr 21:1

DAVID THE FORERUNNER

'I am confident of this, that the one who began a good work among you will bring it to completion by the day of Jesus Christ.'[1]

2 SAMUEL 24:18–25

David spoke of his people as sheep (v 17). He was their shepherd and he was desperate to carry the punishment for them. He recognised that kingship is about self-sacrifice rather than privilege and pride. Each time David turned to the Lord in repentance, he heard the word of the Lord and responded in obedience. He now had to build an altar.

The encounter between the dignified and dutiful Araunah, possibly the leader of the local Canaanite inhabitants of Jerusalem, and King David, in a hurry to do what the Lord has commanded, illustrates David's renewed sense of servanthood. He could probably have taken the threshing floor whether Araunah offered it or not, but he could not offer an 'atoning' sacrifice that cost him nothing. So the purchase was completed, the offerings were made, and the Lord heard and answered. This ends the summing-up of David's life.

In a way, it is a small, manageable act – to buy a threshing floor and build an altar to the Lord – but this is a significant place, on a hill above Jerusalem, the probable site of the future temple. This is God's chosen place for his people to worship, pray and make their sacrifices. This is where they will sing the psalms of David, going up the hill in procession.[2] This is where they will know that God is dwelling with them. Later, at the right time, David's greater Son will come and be given the name Emmanuel, God with us. He will fulfil all the covenant promises to David, and the inheritors of the promises will come from all corners of the earth to worship him in the heavenly new Jerusalem, where there is 'no temple in the city, for its temple is the Lord God the Almighty and the Lamb.'[3]

Lord, help us to learn from David to trust you and turn to you in failure and victory, in great enterprises and in small ones.

---

[1] Phil 1:6, NRSV [2] Ps 122 [3] Rev 21:22, NRSV

FOR FURTHER STUDY

Here are some other resources from Scripture Union to help you keep on reading the Bible regularly – in your small group and individually:

Whitney Kuniholm, *Essential 100*, Scripture Union, 2010 – a comprehensive overview of the Bible including introductions for different sections, 100 readings with notes, and opportunities to pray and respond. It encourages a holistic head and heart engagement with the Bible alongside intimacy with God.

John Grayston, *Explorer's Guide to the Bible*, Scripture Union, 2008 – for anyone who wants to know more about the Bible but isn't an expert. The book is divided into three main sections to give readers different levels of Bible engagement, ranging from a general overview to a close-up look at each book.

The *God Moments Together* series: small group study material aimed at busy people who are juggling study, work, family, friends, church... These straightforward outlines will help you to meet with God as you get together with others to read the Bible and pray.

The *LifeBuilder* series: small group study material. Many titles including topical and character studies, Old and New Testament books.

Encounter through the Bible is a devotional Bible guide that can be used any time. It uses some of the best of the *Encounter with God* Bible series to guide the reader through whole Bible books in a systematic way.

As *Encounter with God*, it is an ideal guide for the thinking Christian who wants to interpret and apply the whole Bible in a way that is relevant to the issues of today's world.

- Devotional Bible guide for use any time.
- Whole Bible books using a systematic approach.
- Helps you read through the whole Bible.

Look out for the other guides in the series:

Genesis, Exodus, Leviticus
Numbers, Deuteronomy, Joshua
Matthew, Mark
Luke, John

RRP: £5.99 per title

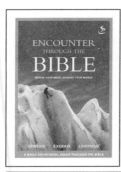 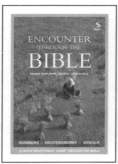 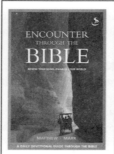 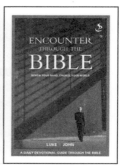

THE WRITERS

DR PHILIP JOHNSTON is Senior Tutor at Hughes Hall, Cambridge and supervisor for the Cambridge Faculty of Divinity.

DR JENNIFER TURNER is a Church of Christ minister, lecturer and writer in Perth, Western Australia.

FRAN BECKETT OBE is a consultant in leadership and governance. She is also leader of 'Restore', an inner-city church-planting inititiative.

MARY J EVANS is a former Vice-Principal of London School of Theology. She is now Acting Dean and Old Testament Lecturer at the Ethiopian Graduate School of Theology in Addis Ababa.

EMLYN AND 'TRICIA WILLIAMS Emlyn is Regional Director of SU's Britain and Ireland Regional Council. 'Tricia is Creative Developer (Adults) for SU England and Wales.

DR DESMOND ALEXANDER oversees Christian training activities for the Presbyterian Church in Ireland. He has written and edited various books, including *From Eden to the New Jerusalem* (IVP, 2008).

DR RICHARD HARVEY is a Messianic Jew who teaches the Hebrew Bible, Hebrew language and Jewish Studies at All Nations Christian College.

REV COLIN SINCLAIR is Minister of Palmerston Place, Church of Scotland in Edinburgh, and Chair of the International Council of Scripture Union.

REV DR WALTER MOBERLY is Professor in Theology at Durham University. He has written a number of books including *The Theology of the Book of Genesis* (CUP, 2009).

REV DR DAVID SPRIGGS is a Baptist minister, and is now serving with the Bible Society as Bible and Church Consultant.

MARGARET KILLINGRAY is a part-time member of the faculty at the London Institute for Contemporary Christianity. She is also a Reader in the diocese of Rochester.

BIBLE READING GUIDES

Scripture Union publishes a comprehensive range of daily Bible guides, both in print and in electronic formats:

Encounter with God: A thoughtful, in-depth approach to systematic Bible reading applied to contemporary living.

Daily Bread: For people who want to explore, understand and enjoy the Bible as they apply it to everyday life. (Also available in a large-print version.)

Closer to God: For people who long to hear God's voice and experience his love and power.

WordLive: an innovative online Bible experience for groups and individuals.

Check it out at www.wordlive.org

SU publications are available from Christian bookshops, on the internet or via mail order:

- www.scriptureunion.org.uk/shop
- info@scriptureunion.org.uk
- 01908 856006
- SU Mail Order, PO Box 5148, Milton Keynes MLO, MK2 2YX, UK

THE E100 BIBLE
READING CHALLENGE

Help your church to be inspired afresh by the Bibl

The E100 Bible Reading Challenge is an initiative to encourage more individuals and churches to become inspired to meet God every day through the Bible – not just for the period of the challenge but beyond.

The challenge is based around 100 carefully selected Bible readings (50 from the Old Testament an 50 from the New Testament) designed to give participants a good understanding of the overall Bib story from Genesis to Revelation. The 'E' stands for Essential and each of the Essential 100 readings ranges from a few verses to a few chapters.

E 100 biblefres
It could change your wor

ESSENTIAL 100
Your journey through the Bible
in 100 readings

Whitney T Kuniholm

To find out more visit:
www.e100challenge.org.uk

The E100 challenge is an initiative of The Bible Societies and Scripture Union movements of Britain and Ireland, along with Wycliffe Bible Translators.

Buy locally at your Christian book shop
Buy online www.scriptureunion.org.uk/shop
Buy direct 0845 07 06 006